Get Rid of Anxiety &Stress

Toby Rice Drews

author of Getting Them Sober

BRIDGE PUBLISHING, INC.

Publishers of:

LOGOS • HAVEN • OPEN SCROLL

Also by Toby Rice Drews:

Getting Them Sober

Dedication

For Ron Lawson

Acknowledgments

I'd especially like to thank the following people for
helping to make this book possible:

Peggy and Ray LaPaglia—I will always be grateful
for them.
                sister and my best woman friend.
     David Nudel, my brother-in-law—with love.
       Claire Murphy—who I love like a sister.
Dr. N. Burton Grace—a powerful example indeed.
Mrs. Liz Brandt—I can't express how grateful
                 I am for her love.
Dr. Edward Kitlowski—my funny, warm, wonderful
friend who has helped me so much.

Foreword

Toby Rice Drews has written another guide to survival in today's world. As in *Getting Them Sober* she has constructed a manual focused directly on her subject and, most importantly, designed specifically and accurately for victims of anxiety themselves. This is a do-it-yourself manual for managing anxiety that doesn't abandon the reader to flounder alone. Ms. Drews seems to come alive through the writing and to stay close to her readers with support, constant new approaches, and a sense of community that transcends the literal messages in her chapters.

She accomplishes this with a style that employs brief vignettes from her clinical experience. These are delicately pertinent to her purpose. They are vivid enough and universal enough to enable the reader to find parts of him (her) self resonating from the examples, thus enabling the readers to be receptive to the messages attached to them. Exchanges from counseling groups are especially vital as the reader is drawn into group sessions and feels the supportive "sharing" that is the strength of the group. Other authors have offered understanding and advice, but Ms. Drews' particular genius lies in her capacity to communicate on paper the intangible qualities of relationships that normally require face-to-face contact. Her words reach out to people and touch them.

Above all, this is a practical manual, drawn directly from real life. As always, real experience cuts across theoretical lines. This is not the usual theoretical treatise in which gaps between real experiences of real people are bridged with constructed concepts. Ms. Drews' thoughts are as varied and diverse as the human experience—there is something real, from real experience, for everyone.

Daniel F. Johnston, M.D., P.A.
—Acting Chief of Psychiatric Service, Baltimore Veterans Administration Medical Center
—Clinical Assistant Professor, School of Medicine, University of Maryland, Psychiatry Department

Contents

Introduction

There have been several books out lately showing us the "nature" of anxiety, telling us about our existential Angst—that we all have it and, therefore, that anxiety is universal. Granted, anxiety is rampant; but do we have to feel that it must be our constant companion simply because the world "isn't just right"? I think not.

Furthermore, the literature does not even touch on the kinds of acute anxiety—anxiety attacks—that plague over twenty million people in the U.S. alone.

What are these anxiety attacks? They *are not* vague and floating anxious feelings; they *are* debilitating reactions—panic reactions—to bodily symptoms of stress. You know you are the victim of an anxiety attack when, at any time of night or day, you get a distressing feeling, or sensation, in your body; you get terrified that this is a symptom of a fatal problem; and you are sure that you are going to die from it, either right now or tomorrow or the next day.

What can this book do for you? It includes hundreds of case histories of clients who have had problems with anxiety and stress—and how they've successfully dealt with these problems—to the point of total cure. By "watching" these individuals overcome their problems, you will learn how to defeat anxiety and stress in your life.

Along with acute anxiety attacks and how to handle them, I've included chapters and case histories on secondary problems. These are problems that make for "regular" anxiety, albeit a great deal of it. A discussion of secondary problems is included so that the individual with anxiety attacks can learn to deal with these problems, to prevent them from getting blown out of proportion. These secondary problems can throw you so out of kilter that just having them will cause an anxiety attack to occur. In other words, I feel a person with this disease must learn how to deal with both kinds of anxiety: the kind that arises from living problems, and the acute type that sends you to the emergency ward.

How can you best use this book? First, look over the table of contents, and read specific chapters that deal with your individual problem(s). Then go ahead with the other subjects—even the ones you do not think apply to your life today. Later in your life you may come across these difficulties, and knowing how to handle them—by nipping them in the bud—will prevent them from blowing up into an internal holocaust; and will, therefore, prevent future major anxiety attacks.

You *do* have the power to recover. As you'll see from your reading, it involves a change in your way of thinking; a change in your attitude toward your problem. And as you begin to *want* to change your thinking, that, in itself, will open the door to changed thinking—and will begin, immediately, to alleviate those painful feelings.

1

Your Nervous System

Your nervous system consists of two main parts: the voluntary and the involuntary.

The voluntary nervous system controls the movements of your head, arms, legs, and body. We more or less control them voluntarily—hence the name.

The involuntary nervous system controls the body's inner functions, including the endocrine system—which controls our body's reaction to stress.

When we are confronted by stressful situations, our endocrine system puts out adrenalin, which is released at the nerve terminals. This allows us to have the extra energy we need to fight, or to run from a situation.

But, when we don't use this energy—when we sit still—that extra energy has to *do* something. And, often, it *does* something like grabbing our stomachs, making our hearts race, making our hands sweat. In other words, if the adrenalin can't fight off our enemies, it will fight our "innards."

An anxiety attack is a result of thoughts about the bodily sensations that occur when you have a lot of adrenalin flowing. It happens like this:

1. A thought comes into your head, even unconsciously, that causes fear about a situation.

1

2. The adrenalin starts flowing in your body, to ward off the feared thing.

3. You get a tightness in your chest, or sweaty palms, or nausea, or a churning stomach, or dizziness; your mouth may get dry, you may need to go to the bathroom—quickly.

4. You don't see the connection between these sudden sensations and adrenalin. *Instead, you think there's something organically wrong with you and that it will be fatal immediately.*

5. You get even more frightened.

6. Your body puts out more adrenalin, to fight off this new fear.

7. You get more disturbing body sensations.

8. You become even more afraid.

9. The vicious cycle continues.

What can you do to stop feeling this way?

1. Change number 4 above. In other words, stop believing that there's something wrong with you just because you're dizzy. Remember to tell yourself that it's just the adrenalin.

2. This will give your body a much-needed "break." As soon as you start to remember the facts about adrenalin, your body will automatically begin to relax a bit, and stop pumping out adrenalin. Some of the symptoms will begin to ease up.

3. When you've got this slight hold on yourself, start to tell yourself that you want to begin to *accept the symptoms, no matter how scary they are.* I didn't say that you have to immediately accept all of them; just tell yourself that you *want* to begin accepting them, and this will unconsciously help your mind to begin to

relax its attitude toward the anxiety attack. It will start to recede; the adrenalin will greatly lessen; the symptoms will really begin to disappear.

4. You must do this over and over again. Only several months of practice will get you to the point of being entirely able to let go of anxiety attacks. For those of you who have suffered from anxiety attacks for years, a cure is only a few months off—and a great lessening of those attacks will begin right away, as soon as you start to use this method!

2

Obsession

Frances had never heard of thought-stopping.

I told her, "Picture a large stop sign—and then say over and over to yourself, 'Stop this thought.' Then get busy doing something else."

"But suppose I *can't* stop?"

"Practice. A child doesn't learn to play a piano overnight," I replied.

"But wouldn't it be better to spend some time, here in therapy, learning about the root causes of my obsession? Then it would be entirely unnecessary for me to have it."

"We could spend years looking for causes. Let's try it this way. It only means a few weeks of hard work, and then you'll be over it."

Frances seemed reassured.

Getting rid of an unpleasant (at best) or paralyzing (at worst) obsessive thought requires only, usually, a few weeks or a couple of months of behavior change. Let's back up a bit, and see why obsessive thoughts are often so closely linked to acute anxiety attacks.

Rachel is a very competent and talented nurse at a prestigious hospital in Baltimore. She's been there for years, drawing a large salary, working overtime on holidays and weekends when necessary. She has long been highly respected by her medical colleagues and loved by her patients.

A series of unfortunate events happened to Rachel, seemingly all at once, over a period of two years. Her husband left her for a younger woman; her mother—to whom she had been very close—died; and her best female friend moved 3,000 miles away to California.

Rachel—being the tough lady she was—kept a lot of her feelings in. She didn't realize the fear and rage she was suppressing.

It started slowly. Rachel started having anxiety attacks. She would start to feel as if she were suffocating; she thought it was a heart attack or angina—those chest pains that came nightly. She went, over and over again, to the emergency room and had EKGs. "Nothing organically wrong," the physicians always told her.

She learned to ignore the chest pains, for the most part. Then a sense of tingling in her fingers, and a feeling of numbness started. Again, she had the doctors look her over. "Nothing," they said.

Not believing them, she went to her family internist, who, for $200, gave her an absolutely thorough physical examination. "You're just fine!" he beamed.

Because Rachel was determined to ignore the symptoms, they subsided for a while.

But then, the thoughts started.

She began to imagine that she would hurt a patient.

The thought came into her mind on a Monday morning. It frightened her, but her common sense told her that she was a good nurse, and so she should ignore it. It went away.

It returned on Tuesday morning. This time, she took an early coffee break, broke out in a cold sweat, and told a friend about it. The friend laughed it off—told her she was imagining things. "After all, you've been a terrific nurse for over twenty years! You could do this work in your sleep!" They both agreed; Rachel felt comforted and went back to work. The thought subsided.

On Wednesday, Thursday, and Friday the thought returned, and Rachel had to leave work early.

She rested over the weekend, determined to "do something about this."

Monday rolled around, and Rachel found herself in a patient's room at 11:00 A.M. About to help this patient start moving some muscles that had been stiff for some time, Rachel had "that thought" again. She broke out in a cold sweat, her mouth went dry, and she was *sure* she would hurt this patient; she feared she would break a brittle bone "by mistake" or tear a ligament.

She got out of the room as fast as she could, calling another nurse to take her place.

It was then she called me. We had been friends in college, some years back, when she was taking a few Continuing Education courses, and I was doing graduate work. She had heard that I was in private clinical practice, and doing behavioral therapy.

"I can't stand this any more! *Can* anyone help me?" We made an emergency appointment for that afternoon.

Briefly, I gave Rachel three guidelines:

1. She would have to learn to *accept* these thoughts for the time being. That in *true* acceptance, they'd go away. Not *compliance*—but *acceptance*.

"What's the difference?" she asked.

"Compliance is when you say, 'Okay, I'll accept this for one minute, or one hour, but they'd better go away tomorrow!' Acceptance, on the other hand," I continued, "is a total acceptance that you may have to live with this for the rest of your life. *The paradox is: when you finally start to really accept it, the disturbing thought begins to recede."*

2. She would have to believe me when I told her that her mind is probably running out of disturbing things to upset her with. And if she applies acceptance to the disturbing thoughts, *knowing that they are just thoughts, and therefore not dangerous*, and if she accepts them as well as the disturbing symptoms, they will subside, and come to an end.

3. She would have to start looking at her anger and fear about being abandoned by three people who meant very much to her, and begin to accept her feelings about that, too.

Rachel is working on the inward journey; but her disturbing thoughts have left, and her symptoms have disappeared.

3

Hysterical Personality

One characteristic of the clinically hysterical personality is that of a person going straight into anxiety, without experiencing the usual fear and/or anger that most people would feel.

Sophie was such a person. A vivacious client, she often described herself as "gorgeously hysterical"—meaning, of course, that she felt it was marvelously theatrical to behave in this manner. What was not so gorgeous, however, was the high price she paid for it.

Whenever anyone disagreed with Sophie, she tended to scream at the person, disdaining any quiet, back-and-forth discussion. She felt it was "her birthright" to be flamboyant. But it was painful, especially in the nighttime, for her.

She almost got a "high" from these discussions. She would invite her friends over for an evening of book discussion and coffee and cakes and all the great delicacies she was known for. Being a terrific hostess and cook, she had mounds of delicious food on the table.

Everything about Sophie was lush. She displayed great treasures from Africa and Spain; her foyer was framed by large paintings from Mexico; her large, oak dining room table was covered, on these occasions, by a lovely red, hand-embroidered Guatemalan tablecloth.

These evenings were a marvel to experience, to be immersed in.

I attended a few of her soirees, and Sophie seemed jubilant; her eyes shone with happiness in response to the intelligence, the vivacity, of her guests. She loved to be surrounded by "people who were familiar symbols."

But the calls I got in the evenings, after these parties, were grim.

Sophie would call, sure that she was dying from something she ate "that was rotten." Or she would think she was having a heart attack. (She was overweight.)

When I suggested, in an early office visit, that she consider actually changing some parts of her life style, she became curious, at first. She wondered what I could possibly be referring to.

"Sophie, you're 'hyped' most of the time. You almost always see things in a black-and-white picture. No grays. People are either 'terrific' or 'backward.' You get angry at people for small things, yet you claim that you're not really angry at them. You say they're 'interesting.' When one of your 'friends' makes a cut at you, even threatens your job—[This did happen to her several times.]—you deny it, saying that the person is just terribly interested in you. After all, how could that happen to you? And you deny you're angry or scared.

"You also think you're a survivor. You've said that a lot to me. Your self-image says that you're not a person who lets *anything* get to her. Therefore, you think you don't *feel* anger or fear like other people. You only allow yourself to 'feel' your feelings when they're so deeply buried, because you won't talk about them. As a result, they overflow into *intense* fear—and since you *still* can't talk about them—they become anxiety. And

10

anxiety, Sophie, isn't a real feeling; it's a cover-up for real feelings."

Sophie, uneasy, told me, "I don't know what you are driving at."

"It's hard to look at this, I know. I'm suggesting that you start to recognize your real feelings about people and situations right while you're experiencing them. *And then put it all into perspective.* Ask yourself several questions:

1. What do I feel?
2. Am I perhaps misinterpreting?
3. If I'm reading it all correctly, how angry or scared would a typically calm person become over this?
4. How important is this—in my overall life?
5. Am I allowing myself to feel contempt before investigating a person or a situation; i.e., am I not seeing why that person may be behaving that way? Can I try to understand why he or she is acting that way?

"In this way, Sophie, you can get some distance from the situation that makes you so upset.

"And there's another important point to look at." (By this time, she was understanding, but looking skeptical.)

"Try to remember that you *do* have a mercurial personality. That you do see things in an exaggerated form—a lot of the time. And that you can be a double-edged sword. Yes, you do experience a lot more joy than most people; but, you also experience a lot more pain than most people.

"Try to see if you can even out your feelings during these bad times. *Ask yourself: what would the average person feel, now? What would the average person think, now?*

"And, then, try to think that way; try to feel that

way. And get busy and drop it."

If you're having problems, like Sophie was, along these lines, and are a little reluctant to give up these intense extremes of emotions, because of the joy you receive when the "good" is going on, try to remember that you can have the pleasure without having all that pain. You can take the edge off the anxiety, and *think* like an average person when the pain gets to you.

And, you may find that thinking and feeling like an *average emotional* person isn't so bad!

4

Living with Exacerbating Problems

Joan was three weeks out of the mental hospital. Her husband was gone; he had left her for good this time, saying, "I can't take any more." With his drinking problem, maybe that was good.

The children were all grown. She still had her best two friends nearby, though. But the house was empty.

Once a week she went back to the hospital for outpatient aftercare. The therapist was a kind woman, a good role model. About the same age as Joan, she was upper-middle-class, and very English. And she was very warm.

Joan liked Monday nights because she could look forward to seeing her therapist on Tuesdays. But Tuesday nights were terrible. It would be an entire week before she'd go back.

Maybe she was discharged too soon, she thought. But the hospital staff agreed that to avoid Joan's becoming institutionalized, she would have to leave, no matter how difficult it might be, and in this way she might learn to cope with the outside world, with all its loneliness.

Sarah was married to a husband who was never home. A merchant seaman, he was gone for six months out of the year. She had three small children, and Sarah felt trapped.

I met Joan while filling in for her therapist who was on a prolonged vacation with her family. Joan was terrified that her therapist was going. I decided that, starting with the first visit, I had to give Joan the kind of advice that would help sustain her through the lonely, long days in between sessions, or she would wind up back in the hospital—not because she needed to be hospitalized, but because she *thought* she needed it.

First, I suggested that she get together a telephone list of people she could call. She was to divide the list into three parts: 1. those persons she could call on to help her during the daytime only, getting their work numbers from them; 2. those who were available in the evenings only; 3. and those who were available around the clock, even if she felt she had to call at 3:00 A.M. Just having that list would help a lot of her terror to subside.

Second, I suggested that she not push herself, but that during one afternoon—or better yet—two afternoons a week she should become involved in being responsible for someone else feeling better. She did this by volunteering at a nearby nursing home. It helped her to forget about her own emotions for four hours, two days a week. At first she balked at this, telling me that she: "would probably be of no use to them as she would be worrying about the lonely night ahead." I told her this just wouldn't happen. And it didn't. As a matter of fact, she gave her phone number to several of the patients, and they often called *her* in the evening and asked for her understanding. This gave her evenings just the uplift she needed.

Next, I suggested that Joan enroll in a class that

14

would give her a job skill—perhaps one that she secretly wanted to learn to do all her life. The next goal was to find a part-time job, within the next six or eight months, and then to increase to full-time, after another year.

Joan learned bookkeeping. She got a part-time job in a small insurance company. She loved the work so much and made herself so invaluable that she was soon asked to take on a full-time job. She asked me if I thought she was able to do so. "Of course," I reassured her.

I had been seeing Joan for over six months, going on seven, when she began working full-time. She was so happy. She developed friendships with older women on the job, and she began playing bridge with them two evenings a week. On two other evenings a week, she went out with a church group. She turned down other invitations because, as she put it, "I need time for myself!"

Joan quit therapy. The last time I heard from her, she was head of the five-woman office staff. She had gotten a $3,000 Christmas bonus; and she took off every Wednesday afternoon to have her hair done.

Sarah's problem was loneliness, and the resultant anxiety that developed. But she wasn't alone—just living in the worst kind of loneliness: that of being very lonely while living with others.

Sarah couldn't stop feeling trapped. She wanted out of the marriage, yet she didn't want to give up her financial security. She didn't want to see her husband when he came home from sea, because she was so angry at him for leaving, although she knew it was his job. At the same time, she didn't want him *not* to come home, either.

She was also ambivalent toward her children. Eventually, she didn't want to care for her three children; but she didn't want not to, either.

She couldn't get out of the double binds she was living in. And she had terrible anxiety and guilt from it all.

The first thing I felt Sarah should do was to see if she could find some way to have her children cared for when they came home from school, so that she could get out of the house and learn a job skill. This would enable her to make *real* choices, later on.

Sarah contacted a free clinic in her area, and they told her of a group of women who were hoping to start an inexpensive, group day-care center for working women.

These women rented a church basement from 3:00 to 5:30 P.M. daily, and began taking care of fifteen children.

Sarah then went to a nearby center—New Directions for Women—and took a battery of tests to learn about her possible job skills. They found that she qualified for work in medical occupations.

A counselor/social worker there got her in touch with a local community college and got her tuition and money for books; she enrolled in an L.P.N. nursing course.

In two years' time, Sarah had an A.A. degree, was a practicing nurse, and decided that she loved being with her children—now that she could be other things, too! She *did* like the things about her husband that she loved when she married him—but, now, she was looking at that marriage from a fresh perspective.

She and her husband decided, together, that he would retire early, after twenty-five years in service, and have more time together.

During the two year period when I worked with her as my client, she experienced a lot of anxiety about the changes she went through. But she realized that this anxiety was better than the anxiety she had encountered when she was doing nothing about her problems. *She decided that if she was going to have pain, it was going to be for growth, not for standing still in her life. And she knew that the pain would eventually leave, if she did something about those problems, instead of giving in to them.*

I noticed that with both of these women, they had had a great deal of anxiety when they weren't doing something about their problems. And when they decided on a positive course of events, they still had these attacks, but *they became less important.* And they paid less attention to them—and, therefore, they faded away.

That's the secret of dealing with anxiety when you are faced with exacerbating problems: Accept the anxiety; deal with problems—and the anxiety will take care of itself. It's letting go of what should be let go of and having the courage to change what you can.

5

Was Your Parent an Alcoholic? A Batterer? A Schizophrenic?

Joni's father was an alcoholic. He died when she was eleven years old—from acute alcoholism. She lived with her four brothers and sisters and their mother, who took in sewing, for a few years, and then started a small business from their home along with their paternal grandmother.

Joni's upbringing was quite strict, especially since her father was an alcoholic. Joni's mother was going to make quite sure that none of the children turned out "like that."

Joni was a quiet, obedient child. She was outgoing only in school, where she had been extremely bright and talented, and where, in her teachers' outlook, she was "too bright not to be bored and therefore talks all the time to the other children who aren't finished with their work." Joni's report card repeatedly said, "Joni talks too much." But she was basically an A student.

Joni had a nervous breakdown when she was twenty-six years old.

Carolyn's mother had been a schizophrenic. Carolyn grew up thinking that it was not unusual for a mother to think that people were talking about her—even the girlfriends who Carolyn invited over to the house after school were accused of "laughing at" the mother.

She thought it was not too unusual that her mother believed people were boring into the household, through the basement. Didn't other people's mothers think that too?

When Carolyn ran away from home at the age of sixteen, to stay at her sister's home in Detroit, she was taken to a girlfriend's house for a weekend when her mother called the police to report her as a runaway. Meaning well, the sister wanted to protect her from the craziness and so she kept Carolyn with her. She was to come back home after the weekend, when the police stopped looking for her. Then she was to enroll in school, and start, for the first time, a normal life.

Carolyn came back to be with her sister after that weekend. She asked: "Why weren't those people screaming at each other during dinner hour?"

Her sister had to explain to her that in normal families, discussions take place; people don't chase each other with butcher knives and fly into rages over imagined happenings.

When Carolyn was twenty-one, she, too, had a nervous breakdown.

Randy's mother always told him that he looked so much like his dad that he would probably "turn out like him." That wasn't so good to hear, as his father was a violent man, prone to beating up Randy and his mother whenever he was drinking—and sometimes when he wasn't drinking.

Randy's memories of his father are clear; he remembers that from the age of seven to the age of nine, when his mother threw his father out, Randy was wakened each morning by the blows of a thick strap. His mother would intervene, trying to stop his father, but to no avail. This would just cause her to get it next.

Randy didn't have a nervous breakdown, but he was in therapy for nine years, and he is still in a lot of emotional pain.

What these children from sick homes who are now adults have in common is that they are still using the defenses they developed in childhood—defenses that helped them to survive those traumatic years. And those defenses are no longer appropriate in adulthood, and they, therefore, cause them pain.

What are some of the defenses that cause such severe anxiety among adults who were victims of battering?

1. A tendency to be always on guard—to be paying too much attention to every word of everybody, taking all that other people say "as gospel." *This keeps up the tension levels for most of the day.*

2. A tendency to make small thoughts—thoughts that most people just dismiss—very important. *Especially thoughts that are negative.*

3. A tendency to put oneself into the double bind. The damned-if-you-do-and-damned-if-you-don't attitude toward almost everything that happens to them. Choices are never acceptable, because *nothing is ever perfect.*

4. The tendency to exaggerate emotions. *Nothing* is ever *just nice.* It's either great or terrible. Fine, if everything's great; but, in life, it isn't always. And the pain involved in thinking that things that are simply unpleasant are *terrible—is* terrible.

A corollary problem is learning to give the problem up! The sheer joy that comes from experiencing such mountains of joy is a difficult "high" to want to give up; but the pain from the lows is a great price.

What are some ways to handle these negative thoughts and feelings that occur, that cause such anxiety?

1. Try to remember that everybody has times when they say things they either don't mean—or they say things that really don't even have any meaning for themselves! Many times if you ask someone who said something that cut into you deeply, he or she may honestly remark, "I don't even remember saying that!" That's how important it was to that person: most often people don't say things to hurt you. *You probably aren't that important to most people for them to be thinking about you, planning ways to hurt your feelings!* (And how good that is to know!)

2. Don't take yourself so seriously, either. Everyone has crazy thoughts, once in a while. You may even decide that these thoughts don't have to be such bugaboos; you could even decide to write a science-fiction story around them and turn them into money!

3. The double bind is a form of perfectionism. *And one form of neurosis is a person who is a failed perfectionist!* (Incidentally, every perfectionist is!) Try very hard to realize that a situation which is *mostly* good for you is a very good situation to be in, indeed.

4. Think hard about leveling out your emotions. You don't have to sacrifice joy, great intellectual discussions, uniqueness, and being interesting to enjoy the emotional calm experienced by most people. That's like having your cake and eating it too! Again, just ask yourself when experiencing the pain of exaggerated emotions, "What would the average person think in this situation?" And, then, *act* on those "average thoughts." You'll have a lot more peace.

6

Surgery After Surgery

Statistics show that the four major diseases of our country are stress-related. A television special in 1978 interviewed cardiologists, neurologists, psychiatrists, internists, and other specialists, about what people could do to cut down on the incidence of disease. Without exception, all the doctors recommended a change in attitude. They especially recommended that people learn how to accept the realities of life and to relax in their attitudes toward life.

Several of my clients have spent more time in the hospital during their adult lives than they have spent out of the hospital.

Karen, a woman in her mid-thirties, is grossly overweight. She has had three stomach operations. Curiously enough, she doesn't mind the trips to the hospital. She says that she considers them a rest from living with her drunk-most-of-the-time husband.

Francine has had a hysterectomy, a colostomy, and several exploratory surgeries. She is only thirty-eight years old. She, too, lives with an alcoholic.

What these women tell me, over and over, along with other women in similar situations, is:

1. They all consider themselves strong women.

2. They all have anxiety attacks. But they do not, as other women might, consider that it makes them "weak." On the contrary, they feel it's normal to have such attacks, considering "how much they have to struggle through in life."

3. They readily admit to anger, even rage. But, they rarely admit to fear.

You might look at the above three characteristics and see, culturally speaking, traditionally male characteristics—except for the anxiety attacks.

What do I perceive in the above? I see women who feel they have no alternative but to view themselves as "above" traditional female reactions. Women who even feel condescending, at best, towards other women who feel fear a lot, and who feel anger not at all. I see them, also, as having contempt for these other "weak" women.

I also see these women as *more* fearful than the women who can show fear. Its analogy would be the terribly macho male who constantly needs to display his muscles and put on a gruff front. How very difficult it must be for him when he is afraid—to have to hide it, not to be able to get it out and deal with it. I see these women as his female counterparts.

But anxiety has a way of catching up to people. You can only "stuff" so much fear.

And, to allow oneself to play the martyr to such an extent as to allow one's body to be constantly mutilated is a "strength" I feel one should be ready to give up. The problem is that these women—and men—often don't feel they have a problem!

Going to the hospital and having friends visit and tell you "you're so strong" may sound nice, but it's not *their* bodies that are being weakened by surgeries. It is truly much stronger to deal with your real feelings than to constantly subterfuge them through other guises.

What can help this type of woman?

1. First, if she does come into therapy, it's often for another problem—not the constant surgeries. Once she is willing to see that her outlook is not perfect, that there are other alternatives to her way of living, she is more willing to see that these surgeries are not healthy. *To break through her rigid outlook on her "strong" way of living is necessary.*

2. This woman must learn to deal with her anxiety attacks in a *surrendering, accepting* frame of mind. Once the fight, the bottling up of feelings, and the female-macho attitude are abandoned, many of the fears will be faced without so much fear.

3. If you are one of these women I have been talking about, and you don't want to enter therapy, but want to change your own situation, you can. *But first, accept yourself as you are. You are a child of God. And be as gentle towards yourself as you picture the finest, gentlest father to be.* And then, some of that gentleness will start to rub off on you. You'll be able to be vulnerable and realize that you won't fall apart when you are vulnerable. And you won't have to be so strong any more that only a knife can reach into you.

7

Crazy-Making Spouses

Diane was living with a man we will call Ralph. Ralph was a recovering alcoholic—but he numbered in the minority in Alcoholics Anonymous. He was one of the few men in AA who merely stopped drinking. Unlike other members, he didn't—maybe he wasn't able to—change his behavior.

Before he stopped drinking, he would taunt his wife, making innuendoes about other women. He would pretend he was interested in them, even when he wasn't—just to get her upset.

Diane went to Al-Anon. There, she learned that if a sober alcoholic still acts like he did when he was drinking, he will emotionally hurt those he is close to.

This is what she heard: "If you exchange spouses with the woman to your right, her husband, who will then be living with you, will be doing the same hurtful things to you that your husband did. Give him three weeks' time, and he will learn where your 'jugular' is, and he will get you there. I know that for years he's been doing the same hurtful thing to his wife, but that's only because she reacted to it. If he sees that you don't react to a given attempt to hurt you, he will drop it. He will try to get you where *your* 'jugular' is."

Alcoholics aren't the only men who are adept at making life miserable for their spouses.

Sheila's husband never drank, he never touched a drop of liquor except at parties or at other festive occasions, maybe ten times a year.

But Dick beat her up, especially when she was pregnant. He threw her down the cellar stairs when she was seven months pregnant. He also slept with every woman he could find—provided they were women Sheila knew.

Both Diana and Sheila "went crazy" as a result of their husbands' behavior.

What Diane discovered was that since her father had been an alcoholic and her mother had been mentally ill, she carried guilt around—an irrational guilt—that she was to blame for not helping her parents get well.

I counseled Diane as follows: "It's all right to know all this, but it doesn't change your behavior today.

"Every night for two weeks pray for the power to forgive your parents for making you feel responsible and guilty for their problems.

"And also, think about these ways in which you can try to get out from under the abuse you're going through:

"1. Accept the reality of the fact that you are being abused. Read books about battered women, and start to identify with their stories.

"2. Think about the fact that there will be pain whether you stay in the relationship or not. The pain of separation will be there if you leave; but the ongoing, chronic pain of staying in that relationship will remain if you stay.

"3. You don't have to make tomorrow's decision

today. But leave yourself the option of having the courage to make a definite decision. You may want to put the idea of leaving on the shelf, remembering at a future time that it is there for you to be able to look at whenever you're ready."

Both of these women had allowed themselves to experience regular pain, inflicted by a person close to them, partly in order not to face the pain—the anxiety—of facing their own lives.

Many women run, get very busy, get involved in outside activities that drain them, get involved with people who use, abuse and drain them, and get involved in crazy-making situations that take up their time and focus their energies in directions that take them out of themselves.

This kind of taking themselves out of themselves is self-destructive.

It's not healthy to turn one's own back on facing one's anxiety—and the inner reasons for it—by either choosing a terrible relationship with a spouse or by choosing draining, mind-bending outside relationships with other people.

Get involved, instead, in helping others without becoming emotionally involved. Learn to cultivate the techniques of inner peace through prayer. Learn to seek the courage to face what's really making you feel guilty or enraged—feelings that underlie anxiety attacks. These ways require facing up to, not running away from, the means to get rid of anxiety and stress.

8

Loneliness

Soon after Malka was separated from her husband, she felt a great relief. She was very enraged, but relieved. Her husband had treated her very badly emotionally; his sexual proclivity towards young children had finally caused her to live in depression, twenty-four hours a day, when she wasn't sleeping.

Finally, she left. She ran out of the house, grabbing a hastily packed suitcase, yelling that she couldn't take it any more. She fled down the street to the house of a friend—a lady who had roomers. She stayed there that night, getting comfort, and being urged on to stay away permanently. She had left him on several other occasions.

The next morning, encouraged by the sunshine, she called her husband. She told him she still loved him, but that enough was enough. She had had it. It was only a year and nine months since they'd been married, but it had been mostly hell, except for the first eight days.

After leaving her husband, she became ensconced in an apartment. For the first six months or so she was there, she didn't have the inclination to feel anything but relief and happiness. She didn't start to date, but would just see her friends, go out to dinner, attend a few movies and church events, and go to work.

After the six months were up, her friends started to grow tired of her needs. They advised her to start divorce proceedings.

She called her husband.

Seeing him one more time just confirmed what she, in her heart, already knew: he would never change. Within two hours of seeing her and professing to miss her so much, he "started" again. He repeated the same stories of how much he couldn't help himself, how he needed to hurt her, how he couldn't help lusting after women who reminded him of little children. She came home, silent and furious.

Determined to get him out of her life, she called a divorce lawyer. The proceedings started. She felt removed from them. It was time to start building a new life, her friends told her.

It was also then that the severe anxiety attacks started.

I first saw Malka three years ago. She had gained an enormous amount of weight, living alone. Whenever she got lonely, she consumed ice cream, cake, cookies. She shopped at the supermarket near her home, telling the check-out person that she 'was having a party' whenever she would appear at the counter with fifteen dollars worth of junk food for the night. She would eat half of it, get nauseous, take a Valium, calm down, eat some more, get sick, and then repeat the process over again.

Malka told me that she probably wasn't that lonely; that she was just a very private person with anxiety attacks and a problem with overeating. I told her that I felt she wasn't in contact with her intense loneliness and that her overeating and nightly anxiety were probably the result of not having enough people around. I added that she was probably more dependent on having other people around than she suspected.

After several months of therapy, Malka came to a decision. She joined a church singles club, had people over two nights a week, and went out for two other nights. The anxiety abated a bit, but not enough.

Malka distrusted people a bit. That was why she didn't want a roommate. She was also a bit fussy about her home; she didn't want somebody "underfoot" or cooking foods she didn't want. We decided to look at the roommate possibility on a balanced scale: were these inconveniences worth it, when having a roommate would mean help financially and provide her with company? Malka decided that the benefits from having a roommate would outweigh the disadvantages.

She put an ad in the church newspaper, interviewed several applicants, and came up with a suitable person. The woman was a few years younger than Malka; an artist (Malka was, too); a graduate student; and a competent cook who was a vegetarian (Malka became one also, incidentally). They got along famously, and Malka's anxiety attacks lessened greatly.

When the roommate went out at night, which was often, Malka had her attacks; she would drive to her sister's house and spend the night, or go a few blocks away to another girlfriend's house. We looked at that pattern in several sessions of therapy.

Malka, it seemed, had trouble just telling people that she needed them. It had to be a catastrophe, or she felt that they would reject her. Hence, she brought on anxiety attacks, not consciously, but unconsciously.

Malka made another decision: to tell her friends that she needed them. She also told them that she would be available for them when they needed her. She started to pay attention to her real inner needs. She didn't

33

ignore them any longer. When she felt she was getting depressed, she asked herself why. She knew that if she ignored that depression, she would pay for it that night with an anxiety attack. She found, upon introspection, that she wasn't having enough fun in her life. She decided to plunge into it. She started going shopping on Saturdays, and eating out afterwards. She would come home then and clean, as usual, but would have a friend over for a small dinner and they would watch television together. Instead of her usual lonely weekend, each Saturday became full of fun. Her Saturday anxieties ended.

Sundays were for church and housecleaning. But Malka added the element of eating lunch out with a friend after attending church. Sunday nights were filled up with company, too.

Malka understood that she eventually had to learn to live alone more, to grow more comfortable with herself, and to learn to enjoy being by herself. But she wisely wasn't rushing it. Getting rid of those debilitating anxiety attacks was more important, at least for right now.

As Malka became happier, each day filled up with fun and friends, she became more peaceful, more used to peace.

If you've been: a) pretending you're strong, living mostly alone and being alone, having anxiety attacks, or b) recently separated and find that you're over-whelmed by loneliness and anxiety—then, do try what Malka did. Learn to fill your days up, one day at a time. Don't try to fill the void all at once. Find your loneliest day; fill it half up with fun and friends. Then, concentrate on one other day. Once you have done this with several days in your week, you'll find that the quality of your life has improved, and much of your depression will have turned to joy and much of your anxiety— your cover-up for loneliness—will have gone.

9

Mercurial Personality

Karin felt high some of the time, depressed and out of sorts the rest; she went through incredible mood changes. She had just gone through a bout of losing twenty-five pounds because she had felt assaulted by her food after she ate it. At other times, she felt a buzzing in her head after things went especially well for her.

"I have these terrible anxiety attacks at night, especially on days when things go well. And if they go really well, it's terrible."

Karin is a writer. "After I sold my nonfiction book, the publicist at the publishing house called me and told me that a radio station wanted to interview me by telephone, and the show would be syndicated in over 150 cities. It was awful that night."

Karin has a mercurial personality. Her skin is so thin that she seems actually to absorb all the vibes around her, constantly. Once, she watched a television movie about a woman who became a saint, and she cried for days. She identified with the lady so much that she "decided" to become a Catholic and try for sainthood. Acknowledging that she couldn't really do this because it would cause her great guilt to leave her own religion, she simply decided to live a saintly life.

For weeks, she would wake up in the morning, and thank God she was alive to serve Him; she would do things for other people; she would read inspirational books; then she would go to bed, thanking Him for her day. Unfortunately, it was all an emotional "fad" for Karin. Two weeks later, she watched another television movie about a woman writer, and she decided to dedicate herself entirely to her writing, totally forgetting her spiritual commitment. She would become a recluse, she determined, and go around the house in tattered jeans, wearing leotards and men's shirts. Her friends worried about her because she would never call them.

Overidentification? That—and much more.

When she's into her recluse life, she has much anxiety. (This is true of many people who allow themselves to become too engrossed in self.)

When she's into a saintly way of living, she has less anxiety.

Is the answer for her to become a nun? Is there another way of life—one that's evenly balanced—that Karin can learn in order to lessen her anxiety?

Intentionally (because I'd seen cases like this before), I asked Karin if her father had been an alcoholic.

Why did I ask her if her father, and not her mother, had been an alcoholic? Because Karin displays great showmanship and great dependence, both signs of being a youngest daughter, the child of a male alcoholic.

"Yes! How did you know he was one?!" she exclaimed.

"Because," I answered, "you are *so* theatrical, so melodramatic in your personality makeup that it indicates this possibility."

I went on to show Karin journal articles about the personality traits of children of alcoholics. They are

36

called "co-alcoholics," because they display many of the personality problems of the drinking alcoholic, including compulsive behavior, obsessions, phobias, and all-or-nothing personalities.

"What can I do about it? And wait a minute, I don't want to drop all of it—just the parts that hurt."

"Well, Karin, you also have the double-edged sword of creativity as your bane. I think you'll have to get used to the idea that creative, artistic people do have thinner skins, more anxiety, than most of us. But, you can cut down on your feelings of isolation about this by realizing, first, that you're not unique. There are about twenty million children of alcoholics who suffer from needing the same kind of attention, and who all resort to the same hysterical behavior.

"One girl I treated used to hold all her feelings in, and then, regularly, she'd faint away. One evening, at a Christmas party, when her little three-year-old daughter was getting a lot of attention, she fainted, and when she awoke, she told me, with some laughter in her voice, that she wanted some attention, too. People who grow up in 'normal' homes realize and know that there are proper ways to get attention—just merely by speaking up and asking for it, in various ways. They get it. But, she didn't know how.

"Karin, I think you should keep a diary of your days. Write down when you get up, what time, and then what you do, when you do it, and how you feel before, during, and after you do each activity. I want you to look for patterns. And I want you to note, also, what your thoughts are when you feel what you do."

Karin kept this notebook for three months. These were her findings: when she was busy in the daytime, doing things she liked with people she liked, and doing some things alone, and when she didn't pile her day up with hopeless expectations, she felt good. When evenings came, and they seemed like they were going to be full, it was okay.

When evenings came, and there was nothing to do, her imagination went wild. She turned inward, without realizing it, and imagined all sorts of bad things happening to her body.

Even if her evening seemed empty, if she knew she had a commitment the next morning that she was looking forward to, she would be all right.

What Karin had to do was program her mind to stay relaxed when she had no commitments. After all, if life is to be lived as it is, one has to adjust to peace and voids.

Karin had to go through a relearning process. She began to program her mind with these thoughts:

1. Life doesn't always have to be exciting.

2. Practice your relaxation techniques every day, so that you can get used to getting your head right into calming down.

3. Use writing, or painting, or whatever makes you feel most fulfilled, to fill up your evenings. But intersperse those evenings with outside activities involving other people, so that depression about: "Oh, poor me, things are always the same," doesn't set in.

4. Accept the fact that you have a mercurial personality—*and remind yourself that you do have that personality trait so that when mood swings hit you, you aren't scared of them. Learn to say to yourself, "Oh, here comes my mercurial mood swing!"*

5. Enjoy and appreciate the artist in yourself. And learn to be grateful for it.

6. Add other dimensions to your life—especially learn to help other people. It will take away a lot of the unnecessary guilt garbage that people with mercurial personalities seem to pile up.

Karin is a lot happier now. She accomplishes much more in a less guilty, less frenzied way. She has mellowed out, accepting herself, and feeling not afraid any more of her feelings or her thoughts.

10

Suppressed Rage

Joyce's mother was paranoid; she used to wake Joyce up in the middle of the night, when she was a child, and tell her to scrub the floors. While Joyce was performing this strange duty at 3:00 A.M., her mother would rant and rave concerning "the aunts who are plotting to steal the grandfather clocks."

Whenever Joyce expressed anger towards her mother's rages, she was soundly beaten with whatever was at hand. Once, Joyce slammed the sliding doors between the living room and the dining room right on her mother. Another time, she picked up an expensive, cut-glass bowl and smashed it—it had been a present to her mother, handed down through the generations. At no time, when Joyce finally exploded and "had it," did her mother get angry. When these big explosions came, her mother responded meekly because they were justified.

But Joyce grew up with these unconscious thoughts implanted deep within:

1. That she was not to get angry, without guilt, unless *so* provoked for *so* long that it finally justified a big explosion. *But only then.*

2. That she was helpless before the rage of the world. (After all, wasn't she a helpless little girl before her mother's rages?)

3. She saw all the anger of the world as rage. She also saw her own anger as rage. This was because in the house where she grew up, anger was never just anger. It was always rage.

Joyce came to me, distraught. She never, or seldom, felt real anger—balanced anger. She felt anxiety attacks when other people felt anger. She would go straight from suppressing her anger, unconsciously, to guilt (also unconscious), to panic.

She also saw other people's angers as rage, directed at her. Killing rage. She always imagined other people were going to kill her; if a taxicab driver looked sullen, he was a killer. If a waitress was tired and crabby, she was a killer.

I told Joyce several things:

1. Point your finger at the supposed "killer." See those other three fingers pointing back? Who do you suppose wants to do the killing?

2. If a person sees the world as hostile, then of course he or she is going to think that he or she is terribly vulnerable all the time. And of course, consequently, one would get very angry about this. And, if you are a person who goes from anger to rage rather quickly and if you feel vulnerable most of the time, you will, therefore, feel angry, then enraged, and guilty about your rage. You will then say it's other people who are enraged at you. There you have your particular syndrome.

3. Joyce had to start with herself: she had to learn to accept the little angers in herself, first. "But," Joyce pointed out, "I never *feel* angry. How do I accept anger

42

when I don't even *feel* it?" I told her that when she starts to feel anxious, to first ask herself if she's in a situation in which an average person would feel anger. Tell herself, over and over, that it's okay for her to feel anger about that. That it won't hurt anybody for her to feel a little anger.

4. I told her to use any ploy that would work. Joyce decided to see her rabbi whom she hadn't seen since she was a child. She talked to him and *got permission* to feel angry.

5. Joyce saw this rabbi another few times to discuss her probable anger at her mother for making her like she is. After a few visits, Joyce learned to forgive her mother, and to become detached from her, emotionally. At first, Joyce had felt silly about seeing a rabbi; but she felt her needs came first. She decided that she "needed permission" to get all that junk out.

6. Joyce decided, in therapy, to start acting as if the world had less harmful power over her—even less power over her moods, period. She started realizing that she is a capable and strong woman, and no longer the little girl whose mother had terrible power over her.

If you have a problem similar to Joyce's—anger you can't get in touch with; a troubled childhood; terrible anxiety attacks at the times when other people feel anger—try the following methods, too:

1. At night, for three weeks, pray for the person who may have physically or mentally abused you as a child.

2. If you feel the beginnings of an anxiety attack, ask yourself immediately: What do I have to be angry about? Really try to focus in on that.

3. Remember your strengths, often. Remember that you are an adult, not a helpless child. You can walk

away from abusive situations—now.

4. There are very few dangerous people in this world. And you will probably not encounter them in your lifetime. Spending inordinate amounts of time thinking that you are in a dangerous situation is time-wasting. You could spend the time becoming even more productive and more competent as the adult you are.

5. Remember that these thoughts pass. If you get busy on something or someone else, you are practicing getting rid of stinking thinking, and you will be the stronger for it.

6. Don't be afraid to talk it out. If you see a counselor, and discuss this problem, it will diminish it, not enhance it, as you may be afraid of. Storing fearsome thoughts up only make them seem bigger than they actually are.

7. Tackle this problem like you would tackle handling diabetes. It is getting in the way of your leading a most wonderful life, and the sooner you get to work on getting rid of it, and make up your mind to start getting rid of it, today, the sooner it'll be gone.

8. You are responsible for your thoughts and feelings. That also means, happily, that as soon as you change your thoughts about a situation, your feelings are changed. Let me give you an example of this: A man was in a crowded elevator and someone kept poking him in the back. He got more and more annoyed, finally getting angry. As soon as he got off, he turned around to give that person a piece of his mind, and the individual turned out to be a blind man, who had accidentally poked him with his cane. Needless to say, the man dropped his anger immediately. Why? Because his *thoughts* about the situation changed. *Feelings change when thoughts change.* This is very heartening

news to a nervous person. Once you can learn to change your thoughts about situations, by learning new beliefs and belief systems—by changing your old ideas—then your feelings begin to change.

11

Paranoid Thoughts

Paranoid thoughts range from one extreme to another. After you clean the sink, for example, and some water with detergent has splashed on your face you may think you are going to die from it, even though you wiped your mouth immediately. Or you may have been on a blind date and were brought to a party: there was no one there whom you knew and you became paranoid when the hostess overcooked your food. You thought she did it on purpose because she had invited your date to the party, not you, and you felt like an intruder.

But what are you really doing—really thinking?

1. You are paying too close attention to what other people may be thinking.

2. You are paying too much attention to your inner self.

Let me elaborate:

As far as the first point goes, you cannot know what another person is thinking. Beyond this, consider other options that person may be reflecting on—options you may have thought of if you weren't in such a nervous state of mind.

If you were feeling good about yourself (and therefore about other people), you might think: 1. That hostess looked at you "funny" because you suddenly reminded her of an old college roommate she misses so much; 2. She was startled because you are so tall or short or very pretty; 3. Something entirely different crossed her mind when she met you: For instance, she may have realized that she had forgotten to put a certain piece of silverware on the table.

People aren't at all as sinister as your imagination can make them.

Now, about the second point—that you are paying too much attention to yourself.

Often, current literature tells us to "look within" ourselves. It is fashionable to think about yourself all the time, and forget about others.

To some degree, this is healthy. But, it is not healthy to take your temperature nightly. It is not healthy to see the world as constantly threatening your well-being.

What can you do to stop all this self-centered behavior?

First, recognize that it *is* self-centered.

This may come as a revelation to many people; and to some, it may appear to be an insult. You may say, "I'm not conceited; I'm not self-centered; I even listen to my friends' problems on the phone. I like other people and I try to help them, to be involved in what's important to them."

Many people fit this description. But, visualize a little child who is only two years old, and who is outgoing and happy except when he's wrapped up in himself. (That's about the age you probably feel when feeling vulnerable to the world. And you get *that* wrapped up in yourself when you feel "attacked" by a "hostile" environment.)

48

When you feel this way, try to tell yourself that you are not two or three years old. You are not a helpless child. You are an adult, and you take reasonable care of yourself so that nightly "accidents" are probably not happening to you. (Who was the last person you know who actually *had* all those bad things happen to them that you imagine happen to you?)

Keep a list of all the things you are afraid may be happening to you. Scrupulously keep a daily diary of all the dire things you expect to happen.

Religiously record every terrible thought that you have. Now date it and keep it for sixty days. (If you want to be extraordinarily thorough about it keep it for six months.) *I'll bet that when the six months are up, all the fearful thoughts you recorded about what other people are doing to you or are planning to do to you add up to naught. I'll bet that none of them have happened.*

The problem with paranoid thoughts is, 1. They are very tenacious and, 2. they lead into anxiety attacks.

How can you end them? By accepting them as "just thoughts." Tell yourself that they are harmless in themselves. One patient I work with tells herself, "Okay, thoughts, here you go again! Well, what are you going to try to scare me with tonight? Do your stuff!" And she leans back and looks them in the eye and smiles and they ease away.

If they go away at that stage, fine. If it starts to lead into another anxiety attack, then meet it on two levels: Accept the anxiety attack (see chapter thirteen, on acceptance); and accept the rotten thoughts.

And try to be realistic. If you have really eaten bad food, you'll know within twenty minutes. So, if a large part of your mind tells you that, logically speaking, you're having crazy thoughts again then just get busy doing something to absorb your mind. When twenty minutes have gone by, you'll realize that nothing is wrong.

Last, and very important: Try to remember that God is your Father and He is protecting you. And the other people in this world are God's children, too, and most are average persons like you and me. And the world isn't as dangerous to live in as Hollywood would like us to think. In fact, it's really a pretty nice place.

12

Agoraphobia and Other Phobias

I once ran a group therapy session in which women dealt with their phobias. One woman was afraid to take a bus trip to Philadelphia with her church group. Another couldn't eat canned foods. A third couldn't live above the third floor. A fourth couldn't take a shower in the house alone.

What did all these women have in common? A focusing in on terrible fears, and an inordinate amount of time spent dwelling on them.

But let's take their fears one at a time. The first woman let's call Ruth. Ruth's problem—called agoraphobia—could be solved very simply. There is a method we use in therapy in which a person does a tiny bit of what he or she is afraid of, then increases it just a little. Gradually he does a little more and a little more until he is doing the very thing he was initially afraid of.

Ruth took a bus trip downtown. When I suggested she start this way she told me she wasn't afraid. So why, she asked, should she start with it?

I told her it was good to start, in this experiment, with something that she had no fear of.

Next, and accompanied by me, she went on a local

bus trip to a suburb. She was a little nervous but excited as well, for we planned to go shopping at that suburb. She treated herself to fifty dollars worth of new clothes as soon as we got off the bus! After that trip she was eager for her next shopping expedition!

We both lived in the same city, so we tried a day trip to a nearby mall. We first took a forty-five-minute bus trip to Washington, DC, then we took a local bus to the mall. Seeing all the wonderful shops, and with 100 dollars in her purse to spend, Ruth was ecstatic.

She became nervous on the way home, though, and expressed guilt feelings about spending so much money on clothes. I pointed out that it was worth the freedom she was achieving and that, if she went to an expensive clinic to relieve her anxiety, she'd be spending at least as much. Wasn't it wonderful to spend it on clothes, instead!

Two weeks later, we took a shopping trip to the discount houses in Reading, PA. We went with a carload of women who were excited about shopping and who were aware of Ruth's problem at the same time, and were sympathetic. The trip was marvelous! At times, Ruth expressed anxiety, but our firm support helped her through it.

The "big trip" was to be an overnighter, but it was postponed. Instead, the same carload of women went to Philadelphia for a day's museum-visiting, shopping, and lunch. Again, we enjoyed a successful trip.

And then Ruth realized that what she was really afraid of, and didn't recognize all this time, was "staying over" in a strange hotel. We decided it would likely be good for her if a lot of us women stayed in the same hotel room together. So we planned one big shopping and cultural weekend for "the girls!"

That did it. Ruth felt comfortable with us and she was able to tell us when she felt scared. With our collective reassurance she came home so triumphant that she wanted to repeat the trip!

Phyllis was the woman who couldn't eat canned foods. Why? She was sure she'd contract botulism.

All of us in her therapy group did plenty of research. We came up with a startling fact which astounded even skeptical Phyllis: Since the 1920s, only three people in the United States have died of botulism from commercially canned foods.

Because she has seen the overwhelming safety record in this, Phyllis now eats canned foods: provided that she first checks the seams for leaks. And she does not eat from dented cans.

Sharon, the woman who couldn't live above the third floor, has physical symptoms when she even visits someone who lives or works above the third floor.

Sharon is going through divorce proceedings. Her lawyer—a successful divorce attorney whose offices occupy the entire ninth floor of a big downtown office building—has floor-to-ceiling windows in his suite of offices. Sharon only visits him in the most dire circumstances. If she possibly can, she consults him on the telephone instead. But if she *must* visit him, she holds her face in her hands and shields her eyes, using her hands as blinders. She told her attorney that she was afraid of heights, and he merely shrugged and said, "Don't look and don't think about it."

Telling a phobic person "not to think about it" is easy. But it is almost impossible for the phobic, who just can't seem to help it.

I counseled with Sharon—and with Joyce, the woman who couldn't take a shower alone. They both seemed to have a worse time of it than the others did. We came up with the following principles. One or another of them is usually successful:

1. If what you're afraid of is not a great fear (let's say it's one of your lesser fears), try to go through with it. (For example, Sharon occasionally visits high offices. But she doesn't force herself to live above the third floor. If she has to visit an office for professional reasons, she tries to go through with it, even if it means staying for an hour. Joyce, on the other hand, is at the stage where she's willing to try to wash her hair while she's in the house alone. Eventually, she would like to wash her hair and shower at the same time. But, for now, she does one at a time. She makes sure she gets up in time to shower before her husband leaves for work. After he leaves, her "homework assignment" from therapy is to leisurely wash her hair while she's alone. Joyce knows what her problem is: ever since she saw a film in which a woman was stabbed while showering, she's been afraid. But recognizing the problem is not enough: Joyce has to go through the process of *proving* to herself that she's an adult, capable woman, even though her feelings tell her she isn't.)

2. Wear a business suit or a competent-looking, professional-looking outfit when you have to go through a phobic situation. *Looking* competent can make you *feel* more competent.

3. Try very hard to identify with other ordinary people who are at this very minute doing what you fear to do but who are not thinking about it at all. If you are afraid of escalators, for instance, and you choose a small one to try out on, look at the person in front of you. Study him and notice his clothes—get wrapped up

in *them* instead of thinking about the escalator. Your ride will be over before you realize it because you will have forgotten about *yourself.*

4. Read the relaxation technique in chapter nineteen (about biofeedback). Practice it once a day. Learn to get into your relaxation technique *while you're going through* a possibly phobic situation.

5. Accept yourself as you are today! Today you are an average person with strengths and vulnerabilities. Too often the phobic person, especially the person who is beset by many phobias, thinks of himself as a mentally ill, hopeless person. He forgets he has many areas in which he is competent. He forgets that most people don't admit to their vulnerabilities like he, perhaps, does. Those "other people" who seem so strong often, when they come up against trying situations in life which they don't want to face (or which they are afraid of) don't *say* that they are afraid. They just shrug and say, "I just don't want to do that." And then they simply go about their business forgetting, and not letting it damage their self-image.

You must learn to do just that. Say to yourself, "Okay, I can't do that just now, or I can't do it comfortably. *So what?* Let's forget it and go on from here."

Stop chastising yourself for what you can't do. Nobody makes progress until they accept themselves for what they are—exactly—just for today.

13

Acceptance

Maritta sat in the chair. She sat forward, tense, making a fist, clenching her hands, gripping her arms. She told me, "I *can't* accept this!"

Maritta was referring to the statement I had made to accept her anxiety attacks, not fight them.

I told her, "Go with them. Let them ease into your body." (When she was a kid, her physical education teacher told her to *accept* the hardball coming into her glove so that it would sting less.)

Maritta told me she felt despair. She felt she could "just die," and she felt these thoughts might go on forever.

I told her that if she learned how to accept them they would start to go away. This may seem to be a paradox, but it is true.

"Think of the worst thing that could happen," I said.

"I would die," replied Maritta.

"Is that the worst thing you can imagine?"

"Yes."

"Then accept it."

Maritta couldn't. Not in that session, anyway. But she eventually came to that point, and then her getting well really started.

Maritta began to see the attacks become less frequent. She didn't see it, at first. She didn't see it happen until I showed her that the pattern in her life was different. She started to have whole days and evenings that were good, and she didn't even notice because they were so normal that she began to expect them. But when I pointed out the pattern of getting better, she began to see it.

Maritta then began to go through another pattern that was typical of people getting better. She began to doubt that her progress would continue: she thought the rug would be pulled out from under her, that the "axe would fall," that somehow she wouldn't get well. Even though this method has worked for thousands of others—who were sicker than she was!—she wasn't quite convinced it would work for her.

The "biggest," the "baddest," the "sickest"—these are words I often hear people use to describe themselves. But it is a malady in itself to continually denigrate oneself like this. To think of oneself as *so* unique that one can't possibly make it is neither healthy nor helpful.

I once heard a true story about an alcoholic who became so mentally, physically, and spiritually sick from the disease of alcoholism that he wound up in a mental hospital for the criminally insane. He was to be institutionalized for the remainder of his life. With proper treatment, however, that man is now out and has been a counselor for over seven years.

One of the first things he had to learn in treatment was to accept himself and his disease. Once he could accept that his treatment was only beginning, he could accept the fact that he only has one day at a time to work with in order to get well.

The same applies to you. You have only today. Work

with it. *And you might as well learn to enjoy yourself while you're getting well!*

One of the slogans which helped the alcoholic man was "Keep It Simple, Make It Fun (KISMIF)."

Maritta was able to do that.

So was Joyce.

Joyce focused on tummy aches, broken fingernails, and toothaches. Each time she got a minor pain (and they truly *were* all minor), she thought she was going to die.

Joyce had read all of the medical books at her nearby library. This would have been a positive step, but she wound up by not believing them. She became skeptical of the three medical opinions she invariably received time after time from doctors. She wound up believing that all roads lead to cancer.

She became frightened, and panic-stricken at night. She spent a good two to three hours per evening on the telephone with friends and acquaintances who were pharmacists and psychiatrists, asking them for reassurance.

When she started wearing out her friends, she panicked and came to see me as a patient. The last thing she wanted to hear was to learn to accept her symptoms.

"But suppose this time it's real?!"

"Maybe this time it is. Let's take that to its logical conclusion. One out of 100,000 times, you might have an infected fingernail. It can wait until tomorrow. Or the next day. *Very few things are physical emergencies.* The most that can happen is that you will get very uncomfortable. But the way you are living now is a living hell for you every night. Do you want to live this way forever?"

I suggested to Joyce that she keep slogans on her

cocktail table in the living room and that she read the slogans and practice listening to the relaxation tapes I gave her.

I suggested she write the following slogans in thick magic marker, on a large sheet of paper:

EASY DOES IT

ONE DAY AT A TIME

LET THE SYMPTOMS HAPPEN

LET GO AND LET GOD

Joyce tried these methods. She read the slogans whenever the attacks happened to her. She played the tapes. But first, she tried very hard to accept that what was happening to her was okay.

"It's okay. What's the worst thing that can happen to me? Botulism only killed three people in the United States in the last fifty years. It's like worrying what would happen to me if a comet struck me down." These were the things Joyce repeated to herself as she worried about the can of tuna she had just eaten. Instead of measuring it to see if it had just the "teeniest" bulge to it, she had to start concentrating on these reassuring thoughts.

It didn't happen overnight, but Joyce is getting better. She now has more good days in her weeks than difficult ones. And the difficult times don't last as long.

Start by trying to accept.

If you can't do that, use this slogan: Make Believe and You Will Believe. Pretend that you *can* accept; go through the motions and, eventually, you *will* accept.

And then you'll be on the road to health.

14

Dialoguing

"One thought seems to trigger another. Each one is scarier. Then I can feel it coming on. Oh, brother, here it comes!" Mary sat there, stock still, frightened. Panicked.

"What are those thoughts?" I asked her.

"It scares me to say them."

"You must. It will help you," I urged.

"I'm scared I'll get nauseous and start gagging again, if I do," she said, holding her face with one hand, rubbing her cheek.

"Take your time."

After a minute or two, Mary went on. "First, I get restless. I want to do something to get me emotionally high. I don't mean drug-high, I mean to do something so the day won't loom ahead so empty. Something that will take me outside of myself.

"Then I almost automatically think of a situation that I can't handle. Like the other day, I remembered that my husband mentioned he'd like to go on a fishing trip by himself sometime. That means that for a whole weekend, whenever that weekend will be, I'll be by myself—and suppose I get an anxiety attack while he's gone?

"Then I went into the bathroom to wash my face and

I was out of the special face soap I use. So I used a commercial deodorant soap on my face. It was the one I normally use when I shower. Then I thought I got some of it in my mouth. I got scared and thought it would make me sick. I imagined I did get sick and thought about nausea and there I was with a full-blown anxiety attack."

When Mary finished telling me this she had calmed down a bit, having opened up and not kept it in.

"Mary," I said, "Let's take this point by point. I want you to try to remember what we're saying, and to say it to yourself whenever you put yourself in imaginary, scary situations. *Dialogue* with yourself. Imagine you're in my office and what you would say, like you just did, and then imagine what I would say back to you.

"Now, first of all, if you want to go out for an afternoon, it doesn't have to be such a big thing. Easy does it. And even if you don't go out, the afternoon doesn't have to 'loom' dreadfully in front of you. *You can change your attitude towards the afternoon.* Picture it as a period of time; say five hours. Sit down and schedule what you will do in those five hours. Then start to do it. One by one, one hour at a time. That way, the afternoon will just have gone by.

"But, suppose you do go out. Try to keep your anxiety level down by not expecting that much out of the afternoon. Don't always be so goal oriented.

"Just try to enjoy the process of the walk you are taking to the place you're trying to reach. Be easier on yourself—have fewer goal expectations in yourself, especially in areas where you don't need to have goals. In recreational, leisure time activities, for example, you don't need goals. You *do* need that time to refresh and relax your mind."

"I never thought of that," said Mary.

"A lot of people put added stress on themselves by goal-orienting their leisure time," I said. "They don't realize that that makes them even less productive when they get back to their work. The body and mind need time to recoup.

"About your husband: let's say he does go on that fishing trip. What you're talking about is not very much confidence in *yourself.* When you're dialoguing, Mary, tell yourself that you *are* competent. Since you've gotten married, you have less confidence in your ability to be alone. You think, therefore, that you're less able to be alone, to stand on your own two feet emotionally, by yourself.

"A lot of women have that problem. They get emotionally dependent on their husbands and they don't realize their own strengths.

"Tell yourself 'If he goes away, I'll have a great time then!' Change your attitude about that weekend. Plan every hour. You don't have to stick to your plan, but have it there as a defense against loneliness.

"Plan to meet girlfriends for lunch and shopping; plan to have your hair done; plan to go to a film; plan to watch some favorite TV shows. Have some people over for dinner and an evening.

"When we have to we can *all* get through situations we thought we couldn't. And it makes us stronger afterwards. Not that it's such a big deal—having to go through one little weekend alone. How big a deal is it? Ask yourself that, Mary. All those years of married life; does it matter so much that you'll be alone for one little weekend? After all, he goes to work every day during the week, and you fill your time there."

Mary visibly relaxed.

"Now, let's take that soap bit. For years, mothers have been washing their kids' mouths out with soap. Now,

63

I'm not recommending that, of course. But getting a little soap in your mouth—even deodorant soap—won't hurt you. Face the reality of what is actually dangerous. Almost nothing that is designed for facial use can hurt you."

What I tell Mary about dialoguing is what is effective with all my clients:

1. Try very hard to see reality as it is. Life is not as threatening as anxiety-prone people often think it is.

2. Remember that on your good days, you see people and situations as nonthreatening. Hence the difference is in *you*, in your attitude.

3. Most anxiety-prone persons are stronger than they think they are.

4. Take your days and divide them up into morning, afternoon, and evening. Now divide those parts into hours in which you will do various things. Taking life one very small segment at a time does help.

5. Give yourself credit when you use various techniques to avoid anxiety and, in this way, get through a scary situation. Instead of letting your self-image dwindle, help to build up your ego by telling yourself you did well. Don't dwell on times in the past when you didn't do so well. Let the past die.

6. Don't worry about how you'll get through tomorrow's problems. You only have today, right now. Tomorrow you may be a lot stronger, since you'll have done better today. Tomorrow, you may be able to get through situations that you couldn't get through today. You didn't get anxiety-ridden overnight, and you're not going to get well overnight. But if you work on a little of the anxiety every day, then a little of your problem is being attacked every day. And you will be building a beneficent circle instead of living in that vicious circle you've been living in.

15

Choosing a Nurturing Partner

In reality, Anna was a very competent human being. She was a college professor and a published writer. But there were some gaps in her personality that she had to learn to deal with.

Anna's parents were child abusers. Anna didn't turn out to be one herself. Instead, she turned out to be a very fearful adult. Her fear of people manifested itself continuously in her personal relationships. This made Anna miserable at least twenty-five percent of the time.

When she got into a taxicab and the cab driver was sullen or he cursed other drivers, Anna would let her imagination run wild—she would think he was going to direct his hostility at her.

When a fellow worker mumbled obscenities around her, or when he glared at her, she was "sure" he was a dangerous human being.

Anna's first husband didn't help things. He was a hostile person himself. He didn't know how not to be a vulnerable person—because he felt so vulnerable to the world. But the difference between them was this: Anna acted out her vulnerability by being afraid; her husband acted out his vulnerability by becoming hostile.

For various reasons, Anna divorced this man. She remarried Saul. Saul was a man who knew himself. He had a good, positive self-image.

When Saul worked at his job and a fellow worker was hostile, Saul at first ignored the person. But if the worker continued, Saul finally told him off.

Afterwards he felt better. Saul didn't carry any fear that the person would retaliate. Saul was confident that the person would "just know" he would up the ante and stop him if he went any further.

Saul taught Anna to stand up for her own rights and to complain when the situation was justified.

Anna learned these principles from living with Saul and from watching him relate to people. The principles include:

1. When a person acts like a bully towards you, he is "protesting too much." When someone is constantly acting hostile he is really very afraid inside, and probably would not actually do anything to you. He is satisfied if you take his abuse and don't retaliate: that way he can continue his little game.

2. You must stand up for your rights if you are to gain self-respect and dignity. This is part of growing up and taking responsibility for yourself. Only with consistent action like this will a person lose his fear of other people.

Through Saul, Anna learned that she wasn't a little abused child any longer. She was an adult, and was capable of taking care of herself. And part of taking care of oneself is complaining to the proper authorities when the situation calls for it.

Anna learned a lot from Saul. But she learned, too, that she had to do these things on her own. She couldn't depend on Saul to "take on the world" for her: If she did, she could create a different problem—that of making herself into Saul's "little girl" if she didn't learn to stand up for *herself*.

These encounters with the world, which Anna used to avoid, caused her some intense anxiety attacks. *But she would have had those attacks if she hadn't encountered these persons—if she had stayed the same. Anna learned that if she's going to have pain, it might as well be for growing. If she grew, she eventually wouldn't need to be afraid of other people.*

When Anna had stayed married to her first husband, who was not nurturing her, she had to contend with too much for her to work successfully on her fears.

"It was just like treading water," she told me. "All I could do was to go to work, come home, and watch some dumb television show to relax my mind, and then get supper on the table. At night, it was pure hell being with him.

"One thing being with him did for me, though, was to take my mind off working on *my* problems and to focus on him and his problems."

She went on, "But since I've remarried, and my new husband is emotionally good to me, I can't blame him for my fears even though they're coming out more, now. Because I can't focus on an external 'him' that I can suffer about, and with, I focus on myself.

"But I'm beginning to realize that I need to focus on people outside myself. My husband is nurturing. He realizes I need to focus on other people who need me. In that way, he's not demanding—he's actually glad when I pay attention to people other than him. When I'm helping them, he's really happy for me.

"That's more than I can say for my first husband, who was jealous when I worked with other people.

"I think that people have to be careful not to expect too much. When you 'get rid of' a bad partner you expect your life to clear up immediately. You think you'll feel terrific and wonderful just because you've found a nurturing partner.

"I think you can get someone who is 'on your side,' who is willing to work with you and not against you. But, at the same time, I think your expectations have to be realistic. That person cannot do your growing for you. Nor can he eradicate all your problems for you. A nurturing partner isn't a wonderful daddy or mommy. He can just walk along beside you."

And if he's willing to do that, that's quite enough— and it's wonderful!

16

Keep It Simple

Angie was upset. Her aunt had died several years ago and the will she had left specified that Angie was to receive $300,000. For six months, Angie was counting on getting the money.

Then she found out that her aunt's children were pulling some legal strings to get $75,000 of it—money that Angie felt was due *her*.

On top of everything, she was in a financial bind herself at the time. She needed to borrow money to live on for two or three months while she worked on a doctorate. She had applied for several loans. Two of these appeared to be coming through.

She felt very anxious when she walked into my office.

"I'm in a double bind. First, I'm really angry about being taken for what I consider to be my money. Second, I could get along on one loan, although it would mean things will be tight. I feel greedy for taking both loans, even though only one has come through so far!"

I told her, "Angie, take it easy! Let's get down to some basics. First of all, if you didn't know about the $300,000—if someone told you that you were 'only' going to get $200,000 from your aunt's will—what would your reaction be?"

"I'd be thrilled!"

"Okay. So why are things different? I'd say you're thinking backwards. Try and be happy with what you are getting from the will. Try to forget that some people are getting some of it. They're only getting a small portion of it anyway, so why get so upset? Is it worth your peace of mind?

"Second, it's really okay to borrow the two loans. Stop feeling guilty about it. The worst that will happen is that you'll have a decent cushion in case you get the flu and can't get around for a week or so. Or if you need a doctor. Just having peace of mind that the money is there is good. The creditors wouldn't loan it to you if they didn't have quite a bit of change just laying around—and you're giving them interest. You're not lying to charitable people who are just going to hand you money; you're making two business deals. Would you judge a person just starting out in business to be a con man if he got two loans?"

"No."

She still looked miserable.

"I'll tell you what I think is really happening, Angie," I said. "I think you're a perfectionist, to start with. You expect everybody in the world to do perfect things and to have perfect reactions so that things will be nice for you. You expect your aunt's children to say, 'Since we already have scads of money, we'll leave it all to Angie, because we want to make the world nice for her.'

"Things just don't happen that way. And the sooner you can learn to adjust to the world as it is—instead of hitting your head against a brick wall because it isn't altogether as you want it—the happier you'll be.

70

"And aren't you being a perfectionist when you want *all* of the money instead of being happy with 80 percent of it?"

I continued. "You're also being all-or-nothing oriented about your own actions. Your ideals are too high. You conceptualize yourself as self-sacrificing and saint-like, and you want everybody else to be the same. And you feel guilty when you're just human and want financial security like everybody else.

"Keep things simple. Pray to accept the things you cannot change, for the courage to change the things you can, and for the wisdom to know the difference.

"From this morning, until night think only of the present moment. You've been anxious because you've put yourself in these terrible binds. You have not been accepting the world as it is. You have not accepted the things you cannot change. You haven't been trying to change what you can—your own attitude about your perfectionism.

"I think good, spiritual therapy teaches people to uncomplicate their lives. People need a simple program to live by—a simple program for complicated, complex people. And, Angie, I think you've just got to learn to unravel some of your attitudes towards how you and other people should behave."

A lot of anxiety can be alleviated by learning to live by simple rules. The golden rule is one such example.

Angie learned that she was only responsible for her own response to situations.

Maybe there was a good reason for her relatives to get that money. Could she live on the goodly amount if she did, indeed, receive it?

Angie finally decided that, since she didn't know all the answers to why things happen, she would just try to accept the good fortune which was hers. She would not cry over the extras she didn't get.

She also decided to be good to herself. And that's part of the golden rule, too—to treat yourself as you would like others to treat you and as you would like to see a good friend be treated.

Angie would like to see a good friend have a financial cushion and, if she were in a position to provide for it, she would even offer one herself.

Angie learned to turn her thinking around 180 degrees so that she could learn to live comfortably, emotionally. Keeping things simple is vital for achieving this.

17

Tranquilizers

There are major tranquilizers and there are minor ones. In the major category are such medications as Thorazine, Stelazine, and Trilafon. In the minor category are Valium and Librium.

Valium affects the exact same brain receptors as does alcohol. If you've been taking an average of twenty milligrams of Valium a week for more than three months, and if you keep on saying "I can get off it if I want to," and if you keep on taking it for any of the varied excuses commonly used, you are probably a "Valium-holic." This is equivalent to being an alcoholic. If a person took a bottle of booze and dried it, then put it into pill form, Valium would be the result! It's as simple as that. (Of course, I'm being facetious here, but the point is that Valium produces a disease extremely similar to alcoholism.)

There are no social Valium takers; there are social drinkers. However, taking Valium over an extended period of time is analagous to drinking alcohol over an extended period of time.

Jane, a good friend of mine who was formerly

addicted to Valium, tells me that she truly didn't know she was addicted. She thought she was merely "habituated"—i.e., mentally addicted, not physically addicted.

Why did she think this? Because she read articles in women's magazines which reported that "all those women" who were addicted to Valium were drinking alcohol along with it.

Then she had an awakening! She read articles which explained that you don't have to drink in order to become addicted to Valium. You don't even have to take more than your prescribed dosage *or even take it every day!* You merely have to be unable to stop taking it after having taken it for an extended period of time.

That's when she first realized she was hooked.

But soon she put it out of her mind, telling herself she could stop any time she wanted to. *If* she wanted to. One night, when she took her prescribed dosage, something new happened. She got anxious again within four hours. That had never happened before. (The pill had always worked for the entire evening.) So she needed more.

She tried not to take it; but she was too scared. She decided to "white-knuckle" it. For three days, she would not take any Valium. But she couldn't stand it. After the three days were over, she gulped down her entire night's dosage in one swallow.

Two nights later, she took two milligrams over her prescribed dosage. (The prescribed amount wasn't enough to quell the anxiety attack.) She got high from it for four hours and couldn't come down. She didn't want to be "drunk" from Valium, she merely wanted to be calm. It scared her so much that she wanted to take more to get down from the high. But she was scared to do anything.

After that evening, she knew she had to get off the

stuff. But she couldn't.

She had many talks with her therapist about Valium and admitted it would be better if she did not take it. Her therapist kept reassuring her that she could get along very well without it. But Jane didn't really believe this.

One Saturday afternoon, Jane was having an anxiety attack. She began to reach for her pill bottle but she didn't want to take any Valium. Instead, she got down on her knees and begged God to help her get off the stuff.

After she prayed, she remembered that she had to do her part. So she put her shoes on and, crying, she prayed that—if she went out for a walk—God would help her run into someone who would help her.

After walking for only ten or fifteen minutes, she ran into an old friend who was a member of Alcoholics Anonymous (hereafter called AA). She told him her problem, and he suggested that she attend the meeting with him—it was only three blocks away and would be held in fifteen minutes.

"But what will they think? I'm shaking! They'll think I'm crazy or something."

"Don't worry about it. Sit near the door. If you get upset, give me a 'high' sign. Wave and leave and, that way, we'll pretend you had a previous engagement."

Jane went to that meeting. She didn't have to leave. Instead, she became calm there. She didn't know what this group had to offer, but it sure helped her that night.

She kept going back. Now she's been off Valium for six months and has been attending open AA meetings to help her stay off.

It's getting a lot easier.

If you want to learn how you can get rid of anxiety attacks you have to be willing to go *through* them. If you take a pill to stop them, you must realize you won't be learning anything. The emotional muscles you need to develop in order to get stronger than the anxiety won't get the workout they need in order to do the job.

And drop the "I'm a strong person" bit. Valium addiction is every bit as much a disease as alcoholism. Don't try to shake it alone. Call Pills Anonymous or Narcotics Anonymous or Valium Anonymous and join one of these groups. (See chapter eighteen for a more detailed discussion of these various helping groups and what they can do for you.) If there isn't an organization of this type near you, go to open AA meetings in your area. "Open meetings" are open to people who may have addictions other than to alcohol.

And don't worry about that word, "addicted." All it means is that your body has formed a way of needing a drug. It isn't from any weakness on your part that your doctor innocently prescribed Valium for you when Valium was not known to be dangerous.

What is important now is that you become responsible enough to take charge of your life. Stop letting a drug control your emotions. Taking charge of your life includes taking charge of your feelings and taking full responsibility for them. That's what a *truly* strong person does.

18

Helping Groups

One thing that helped Corrinne very much when she decided to get off of Valium is that she went to Alcoholics Anonymous meetings. She couldn't be a member because she wasn't an alcoholic. But she could go to their open meetings—meetings which are open to anyone.

The oldest residential alcoholism treatment center in the country is Hazelden. Hazelden treats people for all drug-related problems, including alcoholism. Alcohol is a drug, so alcoholics are treated, as are people on all kinds of drugs.

Hazelden has observed that the contemporary problem isn't just one drug any more—like it used to be. The contemporary problem isn't just alcohol (although it is the most widely abused drug in the country). Hazelden identifies the problem as *sedativism*—attempting to deal with life's emotional problems by sedating oneself. People have tried alcohol, Valium, Librium, and many other addictive drugs to sedate themselves.

Hazelden sends their patients to AA so they can learn to live drug-free lives and so they can learn to cope with life's challenges.

As I mentioned in the last chapter, there are several such groups. These include Alcoholics Anonymous, Narcotics Anonymous, Pills Anonymous, and the new Valium Anonymous. Also, Neurotics Anonymous.

These helping groups have one thing in common: they attack the problems of life with a very positive approach. They treat the total person from a spiritual as well as from a mental-health approach. They see one's malaises in modern-day, anxiety-ridden life as problems that the best of psychiatry and philosophy and spirituality can help.

The basic program of all these groups is the same—twelve principles by which to live. If one were to fully live by these principles, one would never have another anxiety attack.

The program advocates keeping things simple. Work through one day at a time. Become honest with yourself.

What Corrinne didn't understand when she first attended AA was this business of getting honest with yourself. She thought she was a very honest person. But she soon learned that getting honest meant to stop blaming others for your problems. Admit what's really important to you and admit that your pride often gets in the way of your getting well. Admit, also, that there is a power in this world greater than yourself.

Corrinne grew in spurts in this helping group. But she eventually got well.

Josan tried a different tack. Not wanting a spiritual approach to her problems she went to Recovery, Inc.— a self-help group that did not counsel her to get off Valium or Librium or to stop drinking. It merely told her that her anxiety was "temper" and suggested ways she could control her thoughts so her anxiety wouldn't be so pervasive.

Sheila went to group therapy at a nearby hospital clinic. It was only held once a week, however, and this caused a problem because her crises seemed to occur constantly. Sheila's therapist wasn't available for telephone consultation very often, especially not the four to five times a day she wanted to call him.

Sheila wound up at a locally based self-help group, much on the order of Neurotics Anonymous. This group (like NA) encouraged her to call other members of the group when she felt bad. The whole group was encouraged to call each other and to be available to one another by phone.

Here are some guidelines you might want to follow for yourself:

1. First, there is no exclusion clause in therapy. Just because you see a therapist or attend a paid, clinic-run therapy group doesn't mean you can't also attend a self-help therapy. Get what you can from wherever you can get it!

2. How do you find self-help groups? Call your telephone operator and ask for the phone number of the one you choose. If there is no listing, call your local Alcoholics Anonymous chapter. Ask the person who answers if he knows someone who can connect you with Neurotics Anonymous or Recovery, Inc. Often, someone in the AA office can direct you to a referral person who can tell you who to call. Perhaps the group you are looking for exists but has no official phone number yet.

3. It is all a matter of individual preference. If you're a person who needs a lot of personal authority, and you feel more comfortable with a hospital backup then, by all means, go into therapy in a hospital clinic.

If, on the other hand, you desire a holistic approach— with lots of amateur people being there when you need them nightly (and a *free* group, to boot!)—then, try one of the Anonymous groups.

Or, try both.

4. If you want to belong to a particular group (say, Neurotics Anonymous), and there just isn't one in your city, write to their national headquarters. Tell them your situation. Say you are interested in meeting people who could start a group with you.

5. Other groups:

    a. Call your nearest counseling center and ask about groups that may really help relax you. Many such groups utilize music or other therapeutic techniques.

    b. If you are a senior citizen, contact your local senior citizen center. They may already have a relaxation group.

    c. Call the pastoral counseling service in your city and inquire about group therapy.

19

Biofeedback and Relaxation

Renee just *knew* if she could find some way to "nip her anxiety in the bud," she would feel better.

"Why don't we set up an appointment for you at the behavioral medicine clinic for biofeedback?" I suggested.

"What's that? I've heard of it but I don't know anything at all about it. And—does it hurt?" she asked.

"No, it doesn't hurt," I answered. "It's set up on your body similar to an EKG. It monitors your involuntary responses to stress. Then the doctor shows you how to relax various parts of your body as well as your whole body. Then he monitors you again to see if you've learned how to follow the relaxation technique."

We made an appointment for Renee for the following week. She went to three sessions.

For the first session, a psychologist attached cords to her limbs and forehead and chest. He then told her to sit in an easy chair in the darkened room and to just think of "normal" things. He went into the next room and monitored her responses on the biofeedback machine.

Then, he came back and said he was going to teach her how to relax. He had gotten her normal reading of her usual stress level. It was very high: 235, as compared to a person with a normal stress level of 65.

"Let's see if we can teach you to lower your stress level to 65," he told her.

He showed her a basic relaxation technique. Then he instructed her to try it on her own at home during the week. "Do it every day," he said. "And do the autogenic breathing every hour *on* the hour, no matter where you are. This breathing technique will enable you unconsciously to get into your relaxation no matter what the circumstances. Come back next week so I can monitor you again and see how well you've practiced."

Renee did go back the next week. She monitored a stress level of 70.

The week after she returned again and had learned to bring her stress level down to 60.

"Is this how calm people are, generally?! When I go through this routine, I feel like I'm falling asleep, I get so calm!" she exclaimed.

The psychologist laughed. "It's about time you learned how to take it easy on yourself. And, no, you don't have to go to sleep to learn how to relax. You'll eventually find yourself more calm than you've ever been."

What follows is the relaxation technique Renee's doctor taught her:

Find a comfortable, quiet place—a favorite easy chair, perhaps, or a sofa. The light should be dim to create an appropriately restful atmosphere. If at all possible, try to schedule this time period—your "relaxa-tion time"—at a time and place where you will not be interrupted. (Once you have mastered the technique, interruptions will not be so annoying to you. But, for now, you need the time to practice and learn.)

Turn the phone off or unplug it. Wear loose clothing. (Tight clothing is often hampering and may distract you.)

Now relax. Say the word "relax" silently to yourself. Breathe in, slowly and deeply. Fill your lungs with air to capacity—but remember not to strain or overextend yourself. Remember to relax.

As soon as your lungs are comfortably and completely filled to capacity, slowly exhale. Again, say the word "relax" silently to yourself.

You have just taken one deep breath. As a physical and mental preliminary to the actual relaxation exercises which you are about to learn you will want to take two or three deep breaths such as this one. (But no more than three! Too many deep breaths will cause hyperventilation, which is not dangerous in itself but may make you slightly dizzy. Two or three slow, deep breaths are very relaxing, however, and will prepare you for your "relaxation time" session.)

As you sit comfortably, and after you have taken your two or three deep breaths, tense a muscle. (You may wish to tighten your fist, or forearm, or even your biceps.) Observe what the muscle feels like when it is tense.

Now relax the muscle and note the difference.

Close your eyes. Now, slowly, take a deep breath. *As you are inhaling, count to ten.* When you reach ten, exhale. As you exhale, count to ten, just as you did while inhaling.

To gauge yourself properly on this counting technique—(you don't want to count too quickly, and it is often difficult for a novice to judge how fast to count)—you may wish to remember a game most of us played as children.

When playing "hide and seek," those of us who were not "it" naturally wanted enough time to hide ourselves. In order to keep the child who was "it" from counting too fast, we created a rule. The person who was "it" had to count aloud—so we could all hear—and he had to say, "one Mississippi, two Mississippi, three Mississippi. . ." and so on until he reached the number ten. Making him say Mississippi after each number slowed him down considerably. (In some circles, the number one-thousand was substituted for the word Mississippi, as in "one one-thousand, two one-thousand, three one-thousand," etc.)

Although you will not necessarily be counting aloud, the use of this technique from our childhood games will help you to count at the proper speed—not too fast and not too slow.

Now breathe in again. As you inhale, count to ten Mississippi. When you reach ten exhale, using the same technique.

Raise both arms to about the level of your waist. Breathe normally while counting to ten silently. Slowly lower your arms.

Your mind should be reasonably clear of any distracting thoughts. But if such thoughts occur to you, recognize that this is normal and simply focus your thinking on the muscle groups which we'll be discussing. (Don't become embarrassed, or ashamed, or frustrated if you get a distracting thought now and then—in other words, don't try *too* hard. Just remember, almost everybody gets occasional distracting thoughts when practicing these techniques. Simply relax and move on to the next step.)

Extend both arms and clench your fists tightly. Count to ten. Then relax and lower your arms. Release the tension by repeating the word "relax" once or twice to yourself.

Observe how your muscles feel when they are relaxed and compare the difference to the feeling you had when your muscles were tense and tight. As you continue to practice you will become more and more relaxed. Become aware of the feeling you have when you are relaxed.

Now raise your arms again. As you count to ten, spread your fingers wide. Notice the tension. Notice how tight your muscles have become.

As you inhale and exhale (each time to the count of ten), relax your muscles again. Remember to breathe slowly and deeply, but evenly and normally, throughout these exercises.

As you continue to practice regularly you will notice your body become more and more relaxed, day by day—even when your "relaxation time" is over and you have resumed your normal daily activities. This is excellent, and is the natural state you're aiming for.

Take one group of muscles at a time. Begin with your hands, for instance. As you raise your arms, tighten the hands into a fist while you count. Then relax them and lower your arms.

The next time you raise your arms, tighten the muscles in your forearm as you count. Then relax them.

Now, as you raise and extend your arms, flex your biceps. Then relax them.

Each time you tighten and relax new groups of muscles, observe the difference in feeling. Continue counting throughout each exercise.

Before moving on to the next group of muscles, take a deep breath and hold it for a count of five. (If you don't quite make it to five, relax and exhale. After practicing for a week or two it will very likely become easier for you to reach five: those who are more adept count to ten.)

But again, the key word is *relax*. You are doing these exercises for yourself—not for anyone else. There is no one whom you need to impress, no one to whom you have to prove yourself. Certainly you don't need to prove it to yourself—to do so will be to miss the point of these exercises.

Now let's move on. Your facial muscles are very possibly tense without you realizing it. Wrinkle your brow as hard as you can (still keeping your count). Notice the tension you can feel in your forehead. It is extremely tight, isn't it?

When you reach your count of ten, suddenly release all that tension at once. Remember the feeling you had when your brow was contracted? Observe the very different feeling now that the muscles are utterly relaxed. Count to ten as you continue to relax.

Squeeze your eyes and wrinkle your nose at the same time. Breathe naturally and count just as you have been right along. And then relax. Let this extremely pleasant feeling of relaxation pervade the muscles of your eyes and nose as you continue to count to ten.

Next clench your jaw and purse your lips. How taut the muscles can get! Now relax. Let go of the tension. Allow this feeling of relaxation to penetrate your jaw, your lips, your entire face.

You can notice the difference between tension and relaxation almost immediately, even while you exercise. Even so, the feeling of relaxation will increase daily and will be even more noticeable by the end of the week.

Okay. Now bend your head backwards very slightly. Tense your neck muscles. Again, observe how tight your muscles feel. When you reach your count of ten, again relax your muscles. Each time you exhale you will feel more and more relaxed.

Concentrate on relaxing. Try not to think of anything other than how you feel when you're tense and how you feel when you're relaxed.

The Japanese have an expression for this. Translated, it means, "sitting quietly, doing nothing." This is a way of saying that one is simply relaxing and enjoying one's private time alone.

Often, Americans feel "guilty" for "wasting time" when they take time out to relax. But such relaxation time is, quite literally, essential to our well-being and health—physically, psychologically, and spiritually. Genesis explains that God rested after creating the world. And Jesus often retreated from teaching after addressing multitudes of people—many times He sought a quiet place where He could commune with God, away from the hectic pace of everyday activities.

So, to continue, bend your head down toward your chest—not quite letting it touch. (Remember to do this slowly, especially if you are out of practice.) Tighten the muscles in your neck. Again, count to ten. Then relax, while counting to ten. Feel the tension slowly draw out of your neck muscles.

Mentally, reflect briefly on the progress you've made so far. Trace the feeling of relaxation as it has traveled from your fingertips and throughout your hands to your wrists and along your forearms and up along your biceps to your shoulders. Then remember your facial muscles—your brow and nose and cheeks. Then down to your jaw muscles and the back of your head.

Your neck muscles, both in front and behind, feel very relaxed just now. You're making progress!

Now face right. Flex your neck muscles again while you count to five this time. When you reach five, slowly face forward again and relax to ten.

Repeat this exercise facing left this time. Count to five and once more face forward slowly and relax.

Continue to breathe slowly and deeply and evenly.

Arch your shoulders tensely. Notice the tension that extends across your shoulders and upper back. Count to ten. Then relax while you count to ten.

Make certain you are entirely relaxed now—that every group of muscles which we have discussed so far is still relaxed. We don't want to allow the tension to creep back when we have finished with a section of our bodies.

Hunch your shoulders forward. Breathe normally as you flex and count to ten. This same group of muscles which we tightened when we arched our shoulders back are now being constricted in another direction. When you reach ten, relax again. And, again, count to ten.

Now arch the small of your back. Count to ten. Relax. While counting to ten breathe in deeply and then exhale completely. Allow your body to experience a "sinking" feeling as you sink into the couch or easy chair which you're sitting on. Relax entirely.

After a few moments have elapsed inhale again but not too deeply this time. Tense your stomach and contract your chest. Feel the tightness as you count to ten. Then exhale, relax, and continue to count.

Breathe normally. Let all of the tension and tightness drain from you. Notice the feeling of relaxation as it penetrates your upper torso.

Raise your left leg slowly and point your toes. Concentrate on pointing your toes as if you were trying to touch an imaginary wall just out of reach. Tighten the muscles in your thigh and calf muscles. Count to ten as you flex rigidly. Then relax utterly as you continue to count.

Now follow this same exercise for your right leg. Count to ten as you flex and then, once again, relax completely.

Raise your left leg again but this time draw your toes towards your head. Feel the tension, especially in your calf muscles. Count to ten. Then relax.

Do the same for your right leg. Experience the tightness and observe the feeling when you relax.

As you follow this series of exercises daily, observe the feeling of relaxation as it develops and extends throughout your body and increases towards the end of a week of sessions. Study how differently you feel when you are tense and when you are relaxed. From time to time, tell yourself, "Relax."

Conclude your "relaxation time" session by taking two or three deep breaths, just the way you started the session—counting to ten each time you inhale and exhale. Then sit quietly for a minute or two (longer if you feel like it).

Your session is now "officially" over. Try to make a time every day for these exercises, especially during the first week. Whenever you can fit them in is fine—some people do them first thing in the morning; others do them at night; while still others do them at midday. Whatever time is most comfortable and most convenient for you is best.

After the end of one week you will very likely notice a marked improvement. You will feel better and generally more relaxed. But it will be well for you to continue these sessions and allow them to become part of your new life style. Once you include this as part of your normal daily routine you will really notice it if you miss a session or two.

Idea: Reread this chapter, underlining the suggestions (such as "now raise your leg . . . now inhale . . . now count to ten"). You may wish to read these underlined passages into a tape recorder, actually counting slowly, "one Mississippi, two Mississippi, three Mississippi," and so on to ten when the suggestions indicate. Give yourself plenty of time to practice each exercise adequately. When you have dictated the entire session onto a blank tape, play it back and allow it to act as your instructor. Follow your own instructions as you guide yourself through the session.

20

Work It Down

About 7:00 P.M., one evening, I received a call at home from a client experiencing distress. "I'm starting to get very anxious! I can feel an attack coming on!" she cried.

"Okay! Grab your coat and come on over. I'm starting a new group tonight, and it's specifically on ways to handle anxiety. Are you alone?" I asked her.

"I think that's part of the problem," she answered softly but anxiously.

"The group doesn't start till 8:00, but get ready and come on over now. You can wait here for the others," I told her.

They gathered in the counseling room: Clara, a woman in her fifties, newly separated from her husband, who had left her for a younger woman; Dolly, aged fifty, who was seemingly cheerful but full of anxious fears; Doris—the woman who called me—and Stephanie, aged thirty-nine, who had gone through group therapy before but explained that it hadn't helped her. No one in the group seemed to know what to do about anxiety attacks which apparently "come from nowhere," said Stephanie.

"First of all," I began, "let's not make the group part

of the problem. I want you all to feel you can be yourselves here, not have to play a part. That in itself can cause anxiety or, at least, stress.

"Now, why don't you all relax and tell me: Do you want coffee or tea or soda?" They visibly relaxed as they helped themselves to the food on the coffee table.

"Now, ladies, let's get comfortable and realize that we have two hours tonight in which to deal with ourselves. And I want you all to exchange phone numbers and call each other between sessions. That will help increase the benefit from the group, I believe. Do you agree?" They all seemed comforted and cheered by that suggestion, and they immediately started exchanging information.

"Doris," I said to the woman who had called me earlier that evening, "do you still feel the way you did when you called me earlier?"

"No," she answered. "I feel a lot better. I think knowing that I'll have a support system—in addition to our regular session—helped me a lot to calm down."

"Does anyone else want to share?" I asked.

"I do," said Clara. "I often know when it's starting—the anxiety, that is. I'm *sure* it's always triggered by an unconscious thought. No, let me change that statement. It's *often* started by an unconscious thought.

"Sometimes, the anxiety starts when I think about a situation. Like, the other day, I kept brooding about what will happen next summer when I won't have any more money coming in—that's when my husband won't have to give me any more alimony."

"Let me interrupt," I said. "This is November. That is six or seven months away. Do you realize that?"

"Yes, but I still think about it. What can I do about it?"

"First of all make plans for the summer, and then forget about it. Do you know what I mean?" I asked her.

"No."

"Well, make yourself a schedule. I remember that you had told me—I hope it's okay to tell the group—"

"Sure."

"Okay. In individual session, Clara told me that she planned to go to a community college and to enroll for a six-month course so she could become a Licensed Practical Nurse. During that time she'd get tuition and a grant to live on. She wouldn't need all that money in addition to her alimony so she'd save most of it. Whatever she didn't need for mortgage, food, her car, and insurance, she would keep for next summer. That's when she'll need it to finish school. She'll need the money to live on because her alimony will be finished by then.

"Do you know what I would do, Clara?" I asked her.

"No, what?"

"I'd make myself a schedule. I would not put off enrolling in the community college. I'd get the ball rolling, and get the money situation set up.

"Then I'd make a detailed schedule in which I'd list all of the things I need to do about the situation at school: You know, like who to call about getting financial aid. You always have to call people and go sign papers and all that.

"Then, as insurance against having barely enough money to get by, I'd see about getting a fifteen-hour-a-week job on campus. This would help provide extra money in the bank. Get an easy job in the library or someplace where your school schedule can easily be worked around. The job would only be a few hours a week, so you can have time to study. And you'd have that much extra insurance in the bank.

"After all that was arranged, I would make myself a big sign that I'd letter with magic marker in big letters and I'd put it on my coffee table." I told Clara my sign would say:

You've Done Everything You Can: You're in Charge of Efforts, Not Results. Now, Let It Go and Let God Take Care of It.

If I've Done Everything I'm Supposed to Do, Then Everything Will Be All Right. It May Not Turn Out Exactly Like I've Planned, But It Will Be All Right and My Needs Will Be Taken Care Of.

"I'd keep that sign on my coffee table and look at it every time I started to worry," I continued. "And then I'd let it go, get it out of my mind, do something that will get my mind off of it.

"I'd ask myself, 'is this worth an anxiety attack?' And if it wasn't—(not much is),—I'd drop it."

I addressed the group. "I think Clara has made a big step in self-knowledge tonight. She knows one of the major things that gives her anxiety attacks. She is aware of what brings them on. She knows the cause is worry about things in the future and that not planning increases her anxiety. This causes needless worry because it is without action.

"I think you've all got to zero in on what causes each of your own anxiety attacks. For our next session make a list of all the little thoughts you've had that have made you anxious. If you feel yourself becoming anxious, ask yourself what is making you feel that way—what thoughts are you thinking to yourself? What situation are you in? Who have you been talking with? What are you wearing? What is your environment?

"If you recognize that a situation or person is making you anxious, try to get away from it. That helps you to 'work it down,' instead of working it up.

This is a sensible approach to anxiety.

"If you find during your writing, that patterns emerge, then recognize those patterns. See if you can start to alter them—that's working it down. Taking the edge off is the first step towards eliminating anxiety attacks altogether."

21

Keep Fifty Percent of Yourself out of Other People, Places, and Situations

Anxiety-ridden people are usually individuals who get intensely involved.

Francine was a client of mine who experienced a combination of anxiety and depression whenever she was at work, alone, or at home with her husband.

She described the situations and feelings to me. "I teach emotionally disturbed children," she said. "When Billie forgets to take his medicine, he climbs the walls. Other teachers with students like him take it in stride. They get momentarily mad at times, of course. But by lunchtime they're laughing and playing cards with the rest of the faculty.

"*I'm* wiped out. I'm still angry at the children for getting so out of control that the principal had to come in. Or else I'm worried about what other teachers think of me. I wind up vacillating between being depressed about the job or anxious that I'll lose it.

"I'm the same way about the rest of my life. I'm depressed or overtly angry about little things my husband does. Or I'm anxious that he'll leave me some day. I think ahead ten years and worry that he'll die. Then I wish he wouldn't come home today. But if he's late, I'm scared sick and have an anxiety attack.

"When I'm doing my writing, I'm okay. But when I'm finished writing I get anxious because there's nothing to do. My life seems useless. Even my writing doesn't seem to matter at that point. But then I get mad at my husband because I feel it's his fault that I'm upset about my writing.

"I don't mean he doesn't encourage me, because he does. He's a writer, too. But I get a conflict about what's really important to me. If I concentrate on being a wife, I don't feel like I'm a writer. It makes me momentarily happy to have some identity. But it's an ephemeral identity—it only makes me happy for a few moments. But then I get wrapped up in him, and then I feel inferior—not pretty enough. You know what I mean. And I see myself in a cracked mirror.

"Before I met him, I was happy with my writing but terribly lonely." Francine sighed. "Either way, it's a no win situation. It's very depressing. And I think that to create an identity for myself, I get into having anxiety attacks.

"These attacks seem to fill space and time. They draw attention to me. This gets me comfort and a feeling of being taken care of by my husband."

I asked Francine if these anxiety attacks were truly fulfilling.

"No!" she exclaimed. "They're painful! I become like a hyponchondriac. I get panic stricken that I'll die that evening. But it feels so good to get comforted—I feel like a little girl, getting help."

She went on. "But it hurts more than it feels good. And that's why I want to let go of them."

Francine had to look inward in a different way than she was used to. She was looking inside and seeing only the inadequate feelings she had about herself.

She was looking outward to seek approval.

She had to learn to take her eyes off of the situations she was in, and the people she was with. She had to learn to become detached. She needed to learn to look inward in order to find the good inside herself. She desperately needed to learn to love this good within her and to learn to love to live with it.

Sally learned that lesson well. Her husband was an alcoholic. He had just gotten out of an alcoholism treatment center. One evening, they were sitting in the living room. Sally was there, and so was her husband. Also present were Sally's son-in-law and his wife— Sally's daughter. Sally's husband started to pick on their daughter: First for not doing something right as a new mother, then for not doing something else right as a relatively new wife.

Sally's daughter suddenly blew up! "Mom! How can you stand what he says about me? And about *you?!*"

Sally wasn't kidding when she answered that she just didn't hear it any more. She had learned to detach herself from worrying about what he would do— tomorrow and all the tomorrows she used to worry about. Worrying if what he said was meaningful— (She knew it wasn't. She knew it was his disease talking[1])—worrying about whether her daughter would ever learn how to detach herself from his badmouthing. (She knew her daughter was emotionally healthy, basically, and would learn, in her own way.)

By being an example, Sally taught her daughter how to detach.

What is Sally's trick? How does she handle this terribly difficult problem?

Sally learned to look at each situation realistically

---

[1]For a complete discussion of alcoholism and how a nonalcoholic spouse can deal successfully with it, see my book *Getting Them Sober* (Haven Books).

and honestly. Her method:

1. She keeps her mouth shut. When a person makes a remark that hurts her, she closes her mouth and opens her mind—to *think*.

2. She then thinks it through. If there was a kernel of honesty in that remark, she separated it from the messenger and looked dispassionately at the truth. If there was something in the remark that pointed legitimately to her problem, she made up her mind to do something about it—*and she did!* If there were nothing in the remark but viciousness, then she could say it was *that* person's problem, and not hers. And she kept her mouth shut long enough to realize that the hurt would pass—it always does, given enough time. She also knew that if the only reason he said it was to hurt and belittle her, repercussions of guilt would be great enough to hurt him more than they would hurt her.

3. There is justice in the world. Sally knew that if she appeared not to react, he would eventually alter his behavior. She knew he was like a child—if he didn't get attention for his rotten behavior, he'd drop it. *And she'd get stronger and feel better about her positive self-image if she didn't react.*

Learning not to react to others is the beginning of a healthy detachment from the outside world and the problems of others.

And if you are detached from other people's problems, you will have the time and energy to devote to a *healthy* self-centeredness. From this balanced point, you will be able to truly help others. You will become others-centered in a calm, fulfilling way.

22

Slippery Places

It was late autumn. The snow was falling outside the window of my counseling room. It was cold outside, but no one inside noticed it. They were too wrapped up in the conversation led by Rachel.

"I used to be in the Movement. [By this, Rachel meant the politically active student movement of the 1960s.] That is, until six months ago. I've made a decision: no more 'slippery places' for me. Let me tell you all what happens to me when I get involved in things that make me anxious: I wind up at the emergency psychiatric ward in the hospital, getting high dosages of Valium.

"I used to work for the Movement way back in the sixties. Then I had a breakdown. For a couple of years, all I concentrated on was getting well. But I always thought, 'well, someday I'll be able to get back in the Movement.'

"After my breakdown, I felt guilty that I couldn't be politically active any more. I always thought that if I could only be active my life would somehow be meaning-ful.

"So I tried to go back to it. But each time I would get active, it would become too much for me. And then I'd

101

have too much pride to admit that it was too much for me, and I'd continue to do it—until I ended up in the emergency room.

"So a few months ago I reevaluated my life style," Rachel continued. "I had to see what was really important to me. And I began to realize that I was placing the Movement as a higher power to me. I was making it more important than my getting well.

"What I mean is, I *consciously* thought the Movement was so important to me because I was helping people through it. But, *unconsciously*, I was getting an ego trip. I was trying to make that 'thing-outside-of-myself' give me the inner ego-strength I need to get from the inside out—instead of from the outside in, like I was doing."

She went on. "Sure, I need a higher power. And I believe I've found mine—a source of strength that helps me to get my own strength back. But that's not like trying to get my strength by strengthening something outside of myself and then leeching off it, which is what I did in the Movement.

"I like myself better now. I feel more peaceful. I still help others, but in a calmer way. In a one-to-one way. I used to think that doing things on a small scale, on a one-to-one basis, was a cop-out. Now I know that what's important is to get myself well so that I can be of *good* use to other people. Because I'm not really of much use to others until I'm well, myself."

Sasha joined in. "You know, I've never been in the Movement. But I've learned to stay away from 'slippery places,' too. Emotional slippery places, that is."

Rachel interrupted. "The Movement was *my* emotional slippery place. No matter how you cut it, I think *any* place that gets you into emotional trouble or emotional discomfort is a slippery place."

Sasha went on. "I agree. My slippery place was my ex-husband. I was divorced and living with a guy—the same guy I'm living with now. Well, my husband—no, I mean my *ex*-husband—would call me and put a 'guilt trip' on me to see him. He'd say he needed for me to come over and help him with this or that emotional problem. I really felt sorry for him. And I still felt guilty about the divorce. Even though I knew, in my heart, there was a good reason for my leaving him. He was messing around with other women—and other men, too. But I still felt guilty for leaving this poor, sick guy.

"Well, I went over to his apartment and comforted him. I got home and my boyfriend who I was living with was really hurt and jealous. I told him there was no reason to get jealous and all. I really tried to lay a guilt trip on him for not trusting me.

"But after subsequent visits—even though I wasn't doing anything sexually—I got such bad anxiety attacks. And I refused to see them as my guilt for living with one guy and going back and forth to see my ex-husband.

"I would tell myself that I was being good for helping him, and that my boyfriend should understand, and that the anxiety attacks came because I was exhausted and had overextended myself—trying to help too many people at the same time. I lied so much to myself.

"But after the last visit to my therapist, after my individual session," here she wryly nodded to me, "I saw what I was really doing. I was trying 'to have my cake and eat it too.' So I stopped. It's that simple. I just don't want that kind of anxiety any more. It isn't worth the ego trip I was getting from two men loving me. It just wasn't worth it."

23

Forgive Yourself

"I was never really a *bad* person," Mae said. "I always felt guilty, though. Just for *living.*"

"Me, too," Claire chimed in. "My mother always said that God was going to punish me. For *anything.* She was so sick. She'd take me by the hand and take me to the bus stop when she'd be in one of her rages, and tell me that she was going to take me down to the police station. I was only seven or eight years old but she'd tell me they would lock me up if I didn't obey her. I was always made to think I was *so* bad."

"Me too. I think my mother was a lot like yours. My mother was always respected as a good woman by the church community. But she was so strict, she made me feel I was bad about my thoughts. And other than happiness, any feelings expressed in our house were strictly forbidden. If you got hit, you weren't even supposed to cry. She'd say, 'I'll give you something to cry about if you don't stop,'" Mae told us.

She went on. "My mother had a dual personality problem. She was paranoid schizophrenic. And I'm sure that her gambling husband—my father—didn't help. But she always made me feel that the world was a hostile place in which to live and that if I didn't walk a very tight line, I'd be no good."

Claire said, "I always felt that even if I stood up for myself, I was performing a dire sin. If I was anything but obsequious to people, I was bad. I still have to learn to grow up. And being grown up, to me, means that I have to take responsibility for my feelings and actions. That means I have the right to have angry feelings. But I should try not to hold on to those feelings.

"I not only have the right to experience anger, but I don't have to feel guilty about it. After all, I'm just human. I don't have to forgive myself for being angry—I have to forgive myself for *guilt* about anger. I have to learn to say to myself, 'Claire, you are just a person, a person who gets mad. So what? You're like everybody else, a human being. You have feelings. But so what? Feelings alone don't hurt other people—*they* have them, too.' As soon as I start to accept the feelings in me, then I can accept the feelings in others.

"If I accept myself, and all my feelings, then I can be of use to others. I can't be of any use to myself until—and unless—I accept them, first."

Then Mae talked. "I never thought about it like that. What I like about forgiving yourself is that, after admitting some of the things I *did* do that weren't too nice, I can forgive myself. I know I won't do them again. Knowing that, deep down inside, is a wonderful feeling.

"I've had affairs with married men, for example. When I was little, I slammed a door on my mother because she 'got to me.' And I broke a favorite Waterford of hers when she raged at me for hours because I just couldn't take it any more.

"I can now see these incidents as part of the family illness I grew up with. And I see them as part of my rebellion, part of my false pride in wanting to be the number-one hotshot. I was trying to prove to myself that I was more desirable than other men's wives. And I did it basically because I didn't *feel* as desirable as their wives. I can see all that now. I'm sorry for what I did, but I forgive myself."

People who are prone to anxiety attacks tend to be people who don't forgive themselves or others very quickly—not way down deep they don't. They believe they are unique, that *their* guilt is worse—more unforgivable—than that of other people.

They tend to see the world as out of proportion, not only in their anxiety, but in general. In *all* their affairs. What can an individual do to alleviate this needless guilt and attenuating anxiety?

1. Try to stop feeling so unique. You're not the best nor the worst person who ever lived.

2. Try to see God as good. Imagine Him as being the nicest, most gentle, loving parent you can imagine. Wouldn't such a parent forgive his little girl or boy for all the "terrible" things you haven't forgiven yourself for?

3. Believe that you did your best. *Most people do!*

4. If some of your guilt is parental guilt, understand that *all* parents feel guilty. Even the best ones do, sometimes! If there's one "sweat shirt message" that all parents give off, it's "I'm guilty." But you don't have to wear that any more. (The best thing a parent can do is to be a good role model, a positive example to their children. And if you develop into a forgiving person, you'll *become* that role model. Don't you want your children to forgive *themselves* for all their little mistakes? Don't you want them to live emotionally comfortable lives, in order to be most effective? Act like that yourself, now, and you'll be teaching them how to later in life.)

107

5. If you can't believe, then pretend. If you can't yet act forgiving towards yourself, then *act* as if you can. Act like a person who makes an occasional mistake in her relations with others, and then falls, but gets right up again, forgives herself, forgets about it, and keeps right on going. *Get the body there and the mind will follow.* If you act long enough as if you like yourself enough to forgive yourself, then you will wind up genuinely forgiving yourself.

6. There is a major problem in any addiction—whether it pertains to food, alcohol, Valium, or whatever. If you are on a diet and go on a binge one night, *forgive yourself!* That's the *only* way you're going to let that night take on the low importance that it should take on: it's only one night. If you let that night be only one night in your life, instead of letting it symbolize a terrible thing, you'll do well. If you forgive yourself and keep on going (seeing it all as two steps forward, one step back), then you'll be fine. You'll be making progress.

7. How do you forgive others more easily and quickly? Pray for them every night for three weeks. If you can't pray, think of one good thing about that person, and concentrate on that every night for three weeks.

These are sure-fire ways to get that resentment out of *your* stomach.

24

Trust Yourself

"I had a really good day today, you know?" Ruthie sat in my office, wearing a new flannel suit, carrying her attaché case and looking very much the part of the executive.

"I really felt good, accomplishing so much today." She seemed wistful. She paused awhile before she went on. "Sometimes, I feel schizophrenic. Not that I see or hear things," she laughed nervously, looking at me. "But I mean, I feel like two people: half the time, I feel like an accomplished woman—doing more than most women do, actually. The other half, when I'm upset, I feel like a failure because of my anxiety attacks."

"I know what she means," Brenda spoke up. "Take me, for instance. I'm a writer. I write novels. I wrote two this year. I invest my royalties and live off the interest. People look at me and say, 'isn't she successful?' They envy me. But they don't see me at nights, when my husband has to walk me around and around the block while I gag and have a terrible anxiety attack—thinking I'm going to die any minute. This occurs once every week or two."

Ruthie, the executive, spoke again. "Here I've been

earning almost $19,000 a year. And in February, I'm going back to school for a doctorate in business. I'll lose my earning power for two-and-a-half or three years. But I'll have the potential to make over $35,000 a year when I finish.

"Like Brenda, people see me as a girl wonder. But they don't see me having my anxiety attacks. They don't see when I close the doors to my office, so scared that I get on the floor and hold on to the chair leg for support. Intellectually, I know it's 'just anxiety.' But it depletes me. It's really debilitating. And it makes me feel so bad about myself."

Brenda said, "I agree with Ruthie. It *is* debilitating. And it makes me wonder who I really am. Am I the competent writer, the famed novelist? Or am I the weakling, the woman who walks around with her head down, who walks down the street at night with her husband with her hands shoved in her pockets, holding onto rational thoughts for dear life? I know I sound dramatic but, after all, I'm a writer." She laughed, but the smile faded when she continued. "I know that my writing produces a personality. No, it just exacerbates the personality mercurialism. But I don't know what to do about my self-image."

"You know," I began, "I think both of you represent a new kind of woman. Before recent times (where more women are accomplishing things than before), women used to be entirely like you picture yourselves when you have anxiety attacks—phobic, passive, and entirely dependent on men taking care of them and curing them.

"What I think we're going through now is a transitional phase. Women, especially women past their twenties, were brought up to feel partly passive and yet accomplishing.

"I think we can put down some guidelines for looking at yourself in these times. Such guidelines can help resolve this dilemma."

What follows are the guidelines we discussed:

1. Try to see yourself as reflecting the ambivalence of the times, especially if you're a woman. If you see yourselves as part of a large group of women who feel and think and act the same way—as women who feel torn apart as far as their self-image is concerned, then you can stop feeling so unique. And, therefore, you can start feeling less scared about whether you, as an individual, can be helped.

2. Try to see yourself as a whole person, instead of as someone who is fragmented. You *are* as competent as you feel when you are at your best! Believe that. A person isn't a series of component parts. You *can* see yourself as strong in some areas and vulnerable in others. But see this as objectively as you would see a car you were about to purchase. Look at yourself: Take inventory. See what runs well, and then work on the parts that need tuning up. That's all. Keep it at that level. Putting yourself down for not having a perfect machine is certainly not an effective way to run your life.

3. Trust yourself. Trust your instincts. Trusting yourself in your business world led you to success there. Now trust your inner, positive sources of strength at night, too. Especially trust your inner sources of strength when you are having anxiety. When the anxiety attack hits you, remember all the positive things people say about you. Remember your accomplishments. Tell yourself good things about yourself. Reflect that this moment, this little moment of anxiety in your life, will pass. After all, you are basically an intact person. Keeping in touch with, and *trusting*,

your inner resources of strength will help you see the anxiety in its true perspective. Therefore, it won't allow you to destroy a smidgeon of your self-esteem.

25

Make Others Unimportant

"It seems as though I'm always being affected negatively by other people. Not that I feel so bad most of the time. It's just that when I am profoundly affected by others, it's bad," said Jeannie.

"When I read books about the Nazi era, I get very disturbed, even now that it's over. I'm Jewish. I know those books are meant to disturb. But they draw me in a perverse way. I mean I get comfort in thinking, 'at least I survived.' "

Carol interrupted. "I don't personally get affected so much by others on television or through books. But I get really affected when someone seems out of sorts. I get very imaginative—my imagination goes berserk, actually. And I start to think that what I said to someone last week might be affecting her now and that she's mad at me. Then I wind up having an anxiety attack."

Judy said, "You know, I'm getting better at it. Yesterday, I was downtown with my husband, and this woman from work saw me. This particular woman is very competitive with me. She was with her husband, and my husband and I weren't very dressed up. As a matter of fact, we were schlepping around in jeans.

But she was all dressed up with her family, and when she saw us she smirked when she said 'hi' to us.

"Now, that would have affected me badly at one time. It would have thrown me into a tizzy about how we all looked. I would have insisted that we immediately go home to dress up. After bickering about that—if I had my way about it—we would have gone home and changed and it would have wound up too late to go back out. And I would have wound up with an anxiety attack and a migraine headache, about the anger and the guilt I had put my husband through—all because of this woman."

Stephanie said, "You know, I can identify with all three of you. Concerning my co-workers, my neighbors, my boss, my girlfriends, all of them: I worry too much what they think about me—what I am doing, what I am wearing, what kind of car we have, how we live, period.

"Right now, my family and I are going through a transition period. We're restructuring our values. We sold a new home and got a larger home with tons of space for the same money. A friend came over and called me a pig when she saw that we have three bathrooms.

"She was jealous and it just slipped out of her mouth. But after she left, I stewed about it and my temper just boiled. And then I felt so guilty for being so mad. Then I also felt guilty about having three bathrooms when she has three kids and only one bathroom. We have only two kids and three bathrooms. I got anxious.

"Ken and I were wondering whether I should quit my full-time job and stay home to do what I want to do: a series of free-lance, part-time jobs from home. I've wanted to do that for years. I'm a natural-born saleswoman. I have lots of friends who would help me get started. I'm a darned good typist. And I was thinking of combining those two skills or at least using both of them to get two part-time careers going from my home.

"I thought I'd get a salesman's catalog of items ranging from watches to clothes to all kinds of gift items. I could buy them at wholesale for, say, one-fifth the price. Then, by selling them for one-third off the retail price, I'd still double my profit. I could make about a hundred dollars a week, and maybe more, using the party plan.

"But, my best friend seemed very judgmental about this. Not that she said anything outright, but she seemed to be implying to me, 'You shouldn't be making money off your friends. You should be working nine-to-five like the rest of us do, or your life isn't as valid as ours.' "

The group went on about this subject for a two-hour session. If you're having problems similar to theirs, problems that cause you to feel anxiety about what other people think and/or say about what you decide to do for your life, think about these suggestions that the group came up with:

1. Treat others and yourself the same way. If you think that someone else would do better if she were to take on an extra job, but if you are sure that she emotionally can't do that, right now, don't say anything. Grant yourself the same right. If someone thinks you could live your life better if you did it his or her way, assume that that person doesn't necessarily know better than you what's actually right for you. But they have a good intention and are merely making a suggestion. Take it in that vein. Look at the suggestion objectively. If it is a good one, see if you can incorporate

it into your life style. If you can't, or don't want to, then shelve the idea for now.

2. Most of the time, when we feel guilty about not doing what others suggest, we are placing their values above our own. We are not trusting our own judgment. Who's to say that he knows what is best for you? (Turn it around. If you were asked to run their life, you'd probably shriek and say, "I can't do that! I don't know what's best for them in all aspects!" Of course not. Grant yourself the same privilege in regards to others. Stop putting the values of other people higher than your own. It'll give you a constant pain in the neck, always looking up to them.)

26

Accept Death

"It seems that every time I get a *major* anxiety attack, it involves my fear of immediate death," Marian said. "For instance, I get chest pains. I can think it through rationally for a long time, but it always comes down to the same point: fear that I'll die *tonight.* If I could only get over my fear of death, itself, then the power of the anxiety attack would be taken away."

"Yeah, that's true. But who can stop being afraid when they think they're going to die within minutes, or hours?" Adele asked.

"I saw some people who weren't afraid of dying," Clarissa said.

Adele interjected with, "I'll bet they were church people."

Clarissa answered, "As a matter of fact, that's true. But it works for them. *They're* happy."

I asked this small group of intellectual women who, for the most part, were scornful of "religiosity," if they were willing to accept part of what the church people had, if only to get rid of some of their pain.

"I'd have to think about that," Adele answered.

"Would you rather hold on to your intellectual pride

and keep your intense nightly fear—or let go of your fear by accepting some of their 'superstitition,' as you call it?" I asked.

Clarissa spoke. "Well, for me, I feel beaten. I'd accept a voodoo man's interpretation of a tree talking if it'd help me through this. Personally, I'm sick and tired of this terrible fear I have." The others agreed, to different degrees.

I went on. "People in Alcoholics Anonymous feel this way about it: When your problem has you beaten to the point of willing to accept help—even from a source that irks you intellectually—then you'll get the help you need.

"And, for the most part, people who have long-term good sobriety in AA have lost their fear of death. They've learned to inculcate certain spiritual axioms into their daily living which help them overcome their worst fears. These fears they came into AA with— fears that approximate what you are all going through.

"As a therapist, I've worked with and learned from other therapists and psychiatrists. I've also worked with and learned from spiritual leaders. I find it interesting that these spiritual and psychological leaders come up with the same type of advice that one can use to dispel the fear of death."

What are these axioms? Their principles are found in these simple messages:

1. First, try to get a personal concept of a power greater than yourself. It shouldn't be too difficult. Start by assuming that there is a group of people—maybe your therapy group?—that has a strength upon which you can draw. From where *do* you draw your strength when you are anxious or depressed? From a therapist? A helping group? A minister? A good friend? What are you going to do to get help when this friend or therapist

isn't around and you need him or her? Try seeing at least part of the universe as a positive force that you can hook into and draw strength from—after all, the universe *works*, and gets *its* strength to keep on going from *somewhere*.

2. So, the next time you're terrified of death, right at the minute of that terror ask God for help. You don't have to believe totally in Him. And don't worry if it doesn't work the first time. Try it for a few weeks. (If you feel silly about it, just do it anyway. You don't have to tell people you're doing it.) *It works.* And you don't have to understand *why* it works. Utilize, don't analyze. *Are you sick and tired enough of that terrible fear to finally try anything—even something that goes against your entire ego structure?* Isn't it worth it, if it works?

3. Ask yourself if you are *really* at the point of finally *wanting* to accept the fact of death. Do you finally realize that thinking about it nightly, just because you fear it so much, is a terrible way to spend your life? Once you decide to accept death as a fact, instead of railing against it, you'll forget about it and start to lose your fear of it.

If you're finally at the point of wanting to accept its "thereness," you'll stop being terrorized at the thought of it.

4. Realize that all of this will take time. You probably won't get "zapped" into suddenly being totally unafraid any more. It'll be more like two steps forward, one step back.

5. When you do have a little setback—when and if the night comes when all the fears set back in—then sit down and write out all that you've learned. Write all the ideas you learn to put into use on the days and nights when your fears vanish. *The solution to the fear*

doesn't lie outside of you—it is within you. And that's comforting, because all you have to do to remove that fear and pain is to change your thinking pattern during those minutes of fear. Practicing this will help you change your attitude.

27

Take Steps Before You're Ready

"But isn't it better to spend a longer time in therapy, before I actually tackle changing the problem? Shouldn't we first be digging out the root causes of my problem, finding out what makes me anxious? If I learn to stop fearing the one thing I'm afraid of, won't I turn to something else? Isn't it like putting my finger in the hole, hoping the dam won't burst—and every time I put my finger in the hole, something else busts out?" Cheryl sat in my office, looking gloomy at the prospect of "never getting well," as she thought of it.

"Cheryl," I answered, "let's take this one thought at a time. First of all, if you learn to conquer one phobia— no, another one won't pop up, just like that. That's a popular misconception about phobias.

"You don't have to find out the root causes of a phobia or a particular anxiety in order to start doing something to get rid of it. That's a popular misconception, too. In the 1950s it was traditionally thought that one had to go through about four years of therapy, four times a week of psychoanalysis, and about $10,000 in fees, in order to 'understand' the basic problems one had rooted in infancy. Then, and only then, were you able to get rid of the anxieties that burdened you.

"Thank goodness that, today, most therapists understand that if you stop worrying about the patient's childhood history, that if you just work on changing the client's behavior, then the concomitant feelings will change after a short while."

I went on. "Let me tell you about a client I worked with who exemplifies this principle rather well.

Sara was a compulsive hypochondriac. But she was determined to get this bugaboo off her back. She kept a log of her behavior patterns before, during, and after each one of her "attacks."

She noticed a pattern: before she became hypochondriacal in a particular situation, she would pay a lot of attention to any pain. Then, while she was thinking and worrying about the pain, she would call people and ask them if they thought she was going to die— even though she knew it was a question that she had compulsively asked before about the same kind of pain.

What Sara decided to do was: 1. Consciously decide to ignore any pain; 2. stop herself from discussing the pain with anyone else; 3. if she was at work she would continue her work, no matter what— she would not let the pain interfere with what she had to do; 4. if she was at a social function and a pain started, she would ask people about *themselves* instead of focusing attention on herself—by this method, she hoped to get her mind off herself and the pain; 5. she would not fool herself—i.e., not let herself say, "This time it's different, this time it's really a dangerous thing that's happening to me."

What Sara chose to do was very difficult for her. But she was successful. Eventually, Sara unconsciously got tired of trying to sabotage herself. And her unconscious gave in to the way the new Sara wanted to be. Her attacks of hypochondria are a lot less frequent now, and a lot less scary. And the accompanying anxiety attacks are practically nil.

28

Be Good to Yourself

I sat in my counseling office, waiting for the group members to show up. One by one, they came in: Laverne, a woman in her mid-thirties, a divorced mother of three; Terri, thirty-eight, never married but living with a man—no children; Shirley, fifty-five, a tall, statuesque executive who had been divorced fifteen years ago and had been living with a very loving man for over three years; and Roxanne, married with grown children, who was thinking about a second, mid-life career and was very anxious about this.

"Hi! Well, let's stop talking about anxiety. It makes me anxious!" Shirley started off this night's session with a bang!

"I feel that way, too," said Laverne. "Sometimes I'm having a good day and then, when I come to the group session, I feel down afterwards. All it has done is to remind me—"

"That you're sick?" Roxanne broke in, shaking her head.

"Yes! That's it!" exclaimed Laverne. "How did you know?"

"Because I feel that way too, sometimes. I do what

I'm supposed to, and I'm slowly getting better. I'm a good wife. I help my grown children, and have a good relationship with them. I'm taking steps to start my new career, whatever it'll turn out to be. And I'm exhausted!" She threw her hands up.

"Whoa, group!" I interjected. "Am I hearing this right? Is everybody doing their best to get better? Is everyone here tired of sickness? Well, let me say something here. This group isn't here to work you to death! Life is supposed to be fun, too! Let's talk about that, tonight. I think I'm hearing that people aren't putting enough fun in their lives."

"Who has time for that?" asked Laverne. "I come home from work, drive the babysitter home, make supper for the kids, then clean up and go over their homework with them—after I've forced them to do it in the first place! By then, it's time to get the kids into bed. And then I'm too tired to do anything but get *me* in bed. On weekends, I do the shopping, the laundry that's piled up, take care of the kids' clothing and school needs, cook and freeze the next week's dinners, iron, do the floors, take the kids to church. I'm lucky if I have an hour to get in some television."

"I think," I said, "it's time to discuss some psychological homework assignments for this group. Let me suggest some things that are very important for people in the group to do at home this week. And let me hear some feedback from you all about this.

"First of all, Laverne. Your schedule is crowded and your money is scarce. I remember your talking at length a couple of weeks back about friends in your neighborhood who wanted to form a babysitting co-op. Joining it would free you for four afternoons a week until after supper. Just think of what you could do with that time! Especially if you continued to freeze dinners over the weekend. You'd have an extra three hours a day to yourself, and there's so much you could do with your time, then. An exercise class, perhaps? That would surely take care of physical and mental needs. What do you think, Laverne?"

She said, "Okay, I'll try it. I'm so fed up with my tight schedule that I'll try anything. Maybe with some free hours every day, my anxieties will lessen."

I did the same with each member of the group. During the last half of the session, we brainstormed and came up with the following ideas and suggestions about being good to yourself. If you're prone to anxiety attacks:

1. People who are burdened with anxiety attacks are usually guilt ridden and resentment smothered. Not consciously realizing the resentment they have built up, they are *unconsciously* aware of it and feel guilty. Often the resentment is due to overburdening themselves in regards to time, duties, and overly high self-expectations. Unable to stand such burdens, they often feel resentment. With the double-bind they often find themselves in they live in constant guilt about such resentment, thinking of themselves as having high ideals. They feel certain that *they* shouldn't feel any resentment, ever. Hence, the anxiety.

2. In order to lessen the burdens, and thereby lessen the resentment and concomitant guilt and anxiety, start putting into practice the idea of being good to yourself. Do this on a daily basis.

3. Warning: The group felt, at first, that they would feel even more anxious and guilty when being good to themselves! But they realized they would eventually get over it. The "pain" from doing it would wear off, leaving only the pleasure from being good to themselves.

4. Being good to yourself daily would have to involve: a. doing it on a daily basis; b. making the pleasure last at least one-half hour; and c. it has to be something that is pure fun—not housework or something-for-others.

Getting well doesn't have to be all work and no play. As a matter of fact, getting well is *more* effective when it's fun. Remember the acronym KISMIF. When it's time to divert yourself, when you feel an anxiety attack coming on, when having fun could be just as effective as getting involved in work, use KISMIF as a diversionary tactic to keep anxiety at bay. What is KISMIF? *Keep it simple, make it fun* (see chapter sixteen). That's what life is *really* all about.

29

Avoid Excited Misery

Tonight seemed to be a "What if—" and "Have I told you before about—" night.

Susan was furious about her alcoholic husband. "He came home about 3:00 A.M., smashed, as usual. He had promised the children to take them camping today. He promised he wouldn't 'forget,' like last time. Well, I got the kids ready, got their backpacks filled, and got their blankets and tent ready.

"We waited for 'daddy'—he was supposed to be home by 1:00 in the afternoon. We waited. It got to be 2:00, then three, then four. I gave the kids a snack. It got to be after six, and I gave them supper. They didn't want to eat, but I thought it was best, so I made them eat a little.

"I played some games with them and we watched some television after supper. And when their bedtime came, they told me they were sure daddy 'was drunk again.' "

"Susan," I said, "how do you *feel* about all this?"

"Horrible! How *should* I feel?" she answered, slightly shocked at the question.

"No, I mean, how do you feel right now, telling me about this?"

"I don't know what you mean."

"I get the feeling I'm watching a soap opera, and you're the narrator."

She laughed. "I guess it does sound like that. Actually, I guess I'm getting some enjoyment from telling 'all!'"

"That's what I was getting at. You don't look *just* upset. You *look* like you're enjoying telling this sad tale. Does anyone have a comment on this?" I asked.

There was silence for a few minutes.

Judy broke the silence. "I can relate to the way Susan's feeling, I think. When I get into a situation that's just too ordinary, too commonplace, or too boring, I manufacture a bad situation that I can get help for. It's the only legitimate way I know to get the attention I seem to need. And it makes it exciting to have something weird or horrible or bizarre to talk about."

I continued. "I call all that stuff 'junk' and the condition it presents 'excited misery.' Let's look at what it *really* does: You are in a situation that's like a soap opera. You 'work it up' by getting even more involved in it than you have to be, by telling yourself, 'so-and-so needs me.' You become thrilled by the excitement. Then, that night, you get an anxiety attack.

"How can you help in a bad situation without getting into excited misery? I believe that if you calmly give a measured, well-thought-out answer to queries for assistance—distancing yourself from it like a doctor would be—you will be helping without working things up in your mind about it. You will be allowing your mind to stay clam about the situation—thereby alleviating any future anxiety attack over the situation. You'll also be training your mind to stay calm, and you'll get used to a rather constant calm."

The women in the group began to practice what we had talked about in the session to avoid excited misery.

A week later, Susan reported, "It was fine, for a day or two. But you know what? I found myself *missing* the excitement! Life was *dull!* I found myself resenting the therapy, resenting being unable to enjoy *some* part of my marriage—even if it was only in recounting how horrible it is!"

The other women reported similar experiences. Their *heads* told them that a new way of life was necessary in order to cut down on their general tension, and to set the pace to avoid anxiety attacks. Their *emotions* told them that excited misery was "fun."

"Group," I said, "for the time being, it's time to forget what your feelings—your emotions—tell you to do. If your intellect tells you it's time to give up excited misery, then that's what you've got to do.

"I think your emotions are six months behind your intellect. That's how long you've been in group. Your feelings still haven't caught up. But they will. Get the body there, and the mind will follow. You don't have to think your way into good living—you have to *live your way into good thinking.*

"After you've learned to use those long-unused emotional muscles, after you've practiced *living* with calm instead of excited misery, you'll start to *think* differently; and, then, you'll start to *feel* different."

That's the progression of getting well: 1. Change your behavior; 2. your thought patterns will change; 3. your feelings will alter according to your thoughts and your behavior, and 4. a beneficent circle will have emerged—instead of that old, vicious cycle. And, then, you'll *love* living in calm, and you won't miss the excited misery.

30

Help Others

"The other night," Carrie began excitedly, "I had to use the piano of a woman down the hall from my apartment. After I'd been there awhile, I started to get an anxiety attack. I don't know what caused it; it was one of those 'out of the blue' type things. It just came on me.

"Well, I knew the woman was in her late seventies, and she was lonely. She started playing the piano for me, playing all the old songs she knew. She was fascinating! She never had a lesson in her life; she played by ear. Here I was, sitting in a marvelous apartment—she had antiques up to her ears: marble-topped bureaus, claw-footed tables, glass-fronted chiffoniers, oriental rugs, grandfather clocks.

"So here I was, listening to an elderly woman play and talk so that for one night she'd have a little less loneliness. Instead of just wanting to get out of there because I was starting to feel anxious, I decided to stay and keep her company, for *her* to feel better. And, you know what happened? *I* felt better!"

Carrie's discussion was a result of our talking in group about how much better we'd feel if we:

1. Got out of ourselves
2. Gave it away, in order to get better

In the next session, Terri talked about her unique experiences which helped her get well. She had made a decision.

"I had to go on a tour for my book. You see, I'd had a nonfiction book published, and the publisher felt it would make scads of money—*if* I'd go on tour to promote it.

"I was terrified. But I knew I had to go through with it. I kept telling myself I was not unique, that lots of others had done it and that I could do it, too.

"I went to the first city. I went on television, but I was terrified. Afterwards, I was sure that I couldn't go on to other cities.

"Then, a strange thing happened.

"Some friends of mine—a man and his wife—had a little boy who had an accident. He was riding his tricycle on the sidewalk near the street, and a drunk driver ran up on the sidewalk and hit him.

"The boy was in the hospital for quite a while. After surgery, he couldn't walk.

"From then on, the family saw their job as one in which they would try to make their son's life as happy and productive as possible, within his limitations.

"They needed contraptions for him—mechanical things that would allow him to get himself up and around by using his arms and shoulder muscles. But they didn't have any money. And they couldn't raise enough through organizations so that they'd have what the child needed.

"So the parents met with several friends who said we'd like to help. They founded a charitable organization for themselves and for other parents in the same predicament. They asked us to raise funds. For a while, we did all right in our local area. We were written up in our local newspapers.

"Then, someone from another city heard about us. He wrote to us and asked us for help to begin a similar organization.

"So we went there and helped. Then other towns started calling us and asking for help so they could get off the ground with organization and fund raising. We were soon swamped, and we got together a kit to teach people how to organize charities and how to raise funds.

"Within a year, we were called from all parts of the country for help. About this time, I was asked to go on tour for my book.

"It occurred to me that this might be a great way to combine the two functions. The publisher was willing to pay for my train fare and hotels and food as long as I would do one show a day—either for radio or for television. The charitable organization wanted me to go on the road for them and help people around the country organize, but they couldn't help with expenses.

"I talked with the publisher: he didn't care if I did charity work in-between shows because that was my own time. He said that if it got me to promote my book without fear, they would *like* it.

"So—in order to conquer my fears and anxieties about traveling to strange cities, I was able to see my main objective: getting this national charity on its own feet.

"If the tour was just for me and my book, I would have stayed in an anxious state. But once I got outside of myself, and decided that the main thrust of the tour was to be for crippled children, I was able to drop most of the fears.

"How do I feel now? I'm stronger than I've ever been. By 'giving it away,' *I've* gotten more peace."

31

Gratitude

Marie came to see me. She looked as depressed as I'd ever seen her. She described how she felt today:

"Did you ever have two days in a row where you had some good, joyous moments and then they were unexpectedly replaced by depression and anxiety? You suddenly think you'll never pull out?"

I told Marie I'd been that way myself. One of the more recent times was sharp in my memory.

"I was coming home from a meeting with a couple who were good friends of mine," I said. "All of a sudden I felt useless. I thought my life was in a rut. I thought I was probably in a low level depression. It was a despairing time.

"After driving for about twenty minutes and answering them perfunctorily, not really listening to their conversation, I became morose. I thought, 'Here I am, thirty-eight years old, and I have to go through thirty, forty, or fifty more years of this?' I didn't want to die, certainly. But I wanted to live a totally pain-free life. Poor me.

"Then I spotted a billboard. It showed a picture of a happy-looking two-year-old child. The words underneath it were to this effect: 'This little old lady has arthritis.' It went on to say that 250,000 children have crippling arthritis.

"Needless to say, that gave me a jolt. What in the world was *I* complaining about? The only thing wrong with me was that I had to clear out a few cobwebs from my thinking patterns and apply some discipline. And all my imagined pain—caused by my own thinking—would be erased."

A friend of mine has to take ten different blood thinners every night for his arms. He has to wear heavy elastic bandages on his arms every day. That doesn't stop him from going to Africa and the western United States and Canada every year, on hiking and other tours. Sure, he doesn't like spending ten dollars per week on bandages and fifteen dollars per week on medicine; he doesn't like occasional visits to hospitals for treatments even when he's on vacations. But he goes. And he generally enjoys his life.

You may have nervous illness. But no life is entirely pain free.

Members of Alcoholics Anonymous are told that, whenever they see an alcoholic who is still drinking, they should recite the saying: There, but for the Grace of God, go I.

If all that's wrong with you is the way you think, you are very fortunate.

Most people who are nervously ill with anxiety believe they are selfless. They are preoccupied with problems they think are imposed upon them by others. Or they are preoccupied with other people's problems and they want to "help" them.

The last thing they wish to think is that they are selfish.

What is *selfish?* Preoccupation with self.

What is *prolonged anxiety?* Preoccupation with self—

under the guise of *needing* to pay attention to self because of imagined dangers.

Use your imagination. Picture yourself in a battle-field, like Florence Nightingale. Can you see her having an anxiety attack and letting a wounded soldier just lay there? Would she not attend to him if she had a slight fever?

Can you imagine fleeing the Nazis? Trying to get along and survive, helping others survive in a concentration camp, and you start worrying about a hangnail?

Can you imagine working as a volunteer in a children's ward for leukemic children and worrying about a minor complaint of your own?

I suggested to Jane, another patient of mine, that she think about Joni—the quadriplegic woman who paints pictures by holding a paintbrush in her mouth. Jane became so fascinated that she bought the book *Joni*, and read it in two evenings. Those were two nights she spent free of anxiety.

Perhaps you might need to read inspiring books at night. Read books of a spiritual or heroic nature, instead of the spy story you were reading in order to try to fall asleep.

You tell me it's a cop-out to not face your problem? It's a cop-out not to "live normally and read normal books"?

Many people who live normal lives read inspirational and positive-living books all the time! Perhaps the normal people you know do read spy stories before they go to bed. And perhaps they can take the excitement. But, for now, accept your nervous illness and your constant state of anxiety. Perhaps you need to accept the fact that you need to put as much calm into your life as possible.

If you are highly suggestible, you should watch what you read, for now. Include inspiring stories in your reading matter. Make sure that what goes into you is good: your food should be balanced, your thoughts checked, and your friends and reading matter inspired. Stick with *winners!*

32

There's No Bad Way to Get Serenity

"I went through four months of rigorous self-discipline," said Sammi. "Getting up at 8:00 A.M., jogging for a half hour, coming home, writing for an hour, doing my housework and chores, having lunch, going out for fun for two hours, coming home, making dinner, eating, doing dishes, writing again, reading, and going to bed.

"I was 'religious' about all this," Sammi went on. "I felt if I learned to discipline myself into a routine, I'd get well, somehow. I used to think all that getting well entailed was getting used to the world, and somehow fitting into its normal routine. I felt that, if I were more 'routinized,' I'd join the ranks of normal people.

"Then, one day, I just got sick and tired of the routine. Everything went awry. I stopped jogging, I slept late, I did half my chores, we ate out almost every night, and I bought paper plates so I wouldn't have to wash the dishes. By that time, I started to feel some lessening of my anxiety attacks. The routine bit *was* working, but it was driving me crazy! Of course, I couldn't stand the total chaos that resulted from my routine going down the drain. At least, not for long. So, after about six weeks of that mess, I started getting a balanced idea of what I wanted in my life.

"Right now, I have some order and some disorder. But the order isn't compulsive, and the disorder isn't bothersome to my morale. As a matter of fact, I feel pretty good. My life is ordered enough for me to feel like I can sit down at my typewriter and write without feeling dismay when I look at the living room around me. And it's loose enough so I don't feel guilty when I take a half hour or an hour out of the day to watch a television movie I hadn't scheduled.

"It's kind of nice, living like this. There's a lot less anxiety in my life, right now. And fewer anxiety attacks."

"What you did," said Marge, answering Sammi, "seems sane to me. What *I* did to get some serenity, by contrast, seems insane to some people. But, for me, it is sane.

"When I quit my job and threw my boyfriend out, friends told me I was nuts. They thought my boss was terrific and my boyfriend was handsome and charming. Even my mother, who didn't approve of my living with a guy without being married, was upset because I was suddenly left without an income-producing man in my life.

"But nobody understood that my boss was really getting on my nerves and my boyfriend was mentally abusing me. He'd be charming—to everyone else. But privately he'd talk to me like a dog. And he was unfaithful to me.

"I tried to understand the two of them. I kept making excuses for their behavior. I didn't realize how much I was stuffing all these feelings inside of me.

"One day, while driving my car, I couldn't get my breath. I was hyperventilating, and didn't know it. I couldn't breathe in enough air.

"I thought I was going to faint and die. I managed to park my car, and I took a cab to a friend's house. I asked her to take me to the hospital. When we got there, the doctor told me I was merely having an anxiety attack."

Marge went on. "After going on *that* merry-go-round of constant anxiety attacks for two weeks—and I mean every two or three hours!—I decided to see a therapist.

"I came here, and found out that I couldn't stand my situation. Home was unbearable and my job was deplorable. Everything in my life was terrible. So I got my home straightened out, and I left my job. Right now, at least, I can live at home in peace. And I have enough money in the bank to live on for two or three months, so I'll be okay. Everybody thinks I'm crazy, but the anxiety attacks have stopped.

"I went through five years of anxiety attacks before. If it takes losing a job and a boyfriend in order not to go through that hell again, so be it."

Tonight's session seemed to be on ways to get and keep serenity. This was necessary to get rid of those debilitating anxiety attacks. Yet no one seemed to believe that there was only one formula—only one "right" way—to run one's life so that the least amount of stress occurred.

Instead, various methods people have used to get calm in their lives were recounted. Some of these were odd. But they brought the calm so desperately needed.

The methods that helped included:

1. One woman enrolled in a course at Johns Hopkins University's evening program. She was forced to do research. In libraries she found she could entirely get out of herself and forget about the little pains that led

143

to anxiety attacks. Since the library on campus was open until midnight every night, she found nightly solace. (Before this, the hours between 8:00 P.M. and midnight were frightening.) The work was intended to be therapy, but when she got an A in the course, it was a bonus. Finding that it brought her great peace of mind, she enrolled in more courses. Within a year and a half, she found herself loving the program, and her anxiety was down to a minimum. She finished the program, wound up with a masters degree, and is now teaching college—with no anxiety attacks.

2. Another woman did just the opposite. She came from a "push and drive," family who told her she had no limits—she could do anything she set her mind to. She was working on a masters degree, teaching college, raising three children, and being a wife all at the same time. Everyone thought this was marvelous, but she was going crazy. The anxiety attacks were terrible. She quit college and stopped working altogether. Now she's a housewife who sells Avon, and she feels terrific. She says she'll go back to school when the children are older, but there's no rush. (I personally believe this woman will miss the exciting work she had been into and, after a year or two, will go back to school. But I don't think she'll ever put herself back into the overachieving rut again.)

In the course of learning what's particularly good for *your* psyche to lessen the stress in your life and to cut out anxiety attacks, remember this slogan:

There's no bad way to get serenity!

Emblazon it on your heart; make a sampler out of it for your kitchen; or put it on a bumper sticker.

33

Creativity—a Double-Edged Sword

"I'm such a flamboyant person," sighed Brenda.

"Me, too," said Kathy.

"I think that's one of the reasons we've all met," I said, leading a group of artists in a group therapy session. The group had been a byproduct of several other group therapies. Five of the women involved were serious artists, and all seemed to have similar personality problems.

"Who would like to start out the session tonight?" I asked.

They all looked at one another.

I began again. "Christie, how was your week?"

Christie said, "Oh, me? Well, my week was usual— up-and-down like a roller coaster. After I had coffee and part of a soft drink, I got really hyper. I really freaked.

"Then I remembered the test to see if I was okay. I'd get involved in something outside of myself, and see if I could 'come down.' If I could, I was okay. I also tried to remember that if I could turn it all over to a higher power, I'd wind up okay.

"Well, I wound up painting, and got my mind totally

off my problems—and I was fine. Painting or drawing does that for me. It's so totally absorbing. Nothing else works like that.

"Sometimes, though, painting doesn't serve me very well. I mean, I feel a lot of ambivalence about being an artist. My ego gets puffed up when I do a good painting, and then I get guilt and an anxiety attack. Or, when I'm finished with a painting that I worked a long time on, I get depressed, and that seems to trigger anxiety.

"Sometimes, when I get really despairing, I feel like a person living on the outer fringe of society. Then I really feel like a madwoman."

"I feel such empathy with what Christie is saying," said Brenda. Brenda was in her early thirties. She always wore the same kinds of outfits she had worn in the late 1960s. Guatemalan tops, jeans or tweed skirts, tights, leather boots, large Mexican jewelry. She looked competent, unafraid, but her words spoke of the woman under the facade. "Sometimes, I get 'into' my self-image so much, I tend to forget to have anxiety attacks! I have my studio and my gallery. I make enough money off my work to live on. Next month, I'll be selling my stuff up and down the East Coast. So, you see, all is well—right? Wrong. I feel safe as long as I'm in my environment of arty people. But as soon as I go to the grocery store, I'm reminded that there are millions upon millions of non-art persons out there—and a lot of them are hostile to art and to artists! I find myself thinking about them too much, and using my imagination to think of them severely persecuting us. And by then, I'm having a major anxiety attack.

"I *know* I misuse my imagination sometimes—a lot of times. But I don't know how not to. Many times, when I get an anxiety attack, I can curtail it by drawing. But if I did that all the time, I'd be drawing when I don't want to draw. And that would cut into my creativity—it'd be a drawback. What do I do?"

Kathy said, "I don't think I ever told you my story. Since I'm kind of new here, in group, I guess it's time I opened up. I'm divorced and living with a man—another artist.

"I'm studying to be an art therapist. And I do field work this semester at graduate school. I get credit for my work, and I don't get paid, but I get experience in my field.

"Well, now, I'm working with three adults at a community mental health center. They really get their feelings out when they're doing the art therapy. They get out of themselves, and out of their anxiety attacks. But, after they're finished, they see success—in the sense that they finished something 'good'—and they see that they're done. Then they realize they don't have an outlet any more. Then they get anxious.

"And, even though their reaction is more extreme than mine, I identify with them.

"It's a lot like what Brenda said. Art is a therapy for me when I have an anxiety attack, but it also *creates* anxiety."

Patti spoke. "I guess I'm the only nonprofessional artist here. But I can identify with what everyone's saying, especially about art being a double-edged sword. It's more like my artistic *personality* is the double-edged sword.

"I'm up, I'm down, I'm all over the place. But that's the very thing that allows me to be the artist I am. I really believe that we artists have mercurial personalities. It's a price we have to pay."

"I don't agree with that," I said. "Usually, as the therapist, I don't talk about my personal experiences.

But I believe it's fitting, here.

"As some of you already know, I dabble in drawing in my spare time. I'm not bad. I've had a couple of exhibits. And I really love drawing. Like all of you, I lose myself when I get into my art. But I've had to deal with mercurial personality problems, too. And some things have helped me.

"I've had to learn to slow up. In my achievement, I've been in such a hurry to accomplish, accomplish, accomplish, that I sometimes lose sight of of my goal. I just concentrate on feeding my ego with more and more accomplishments. I've had to reorder my priorities and do with a few less things 'I've done' in order to become easier on myself. This, alone, has lessened a lot of anxiety.

"*Everything* used to seem important to me. Realizing, internally, that some things are just not that important was like taking a deep breath and relaxing.

"I've had to learn to accept the peaks in my life, and to stop being afraid of them. Every time something terrific would happen, I would freak. I've had to learn to say to myself, 'Easy does it, girl. In six months it won't be so important. Take it e-a-s-y. Slow down.'

"Sometimes, when nothing else works, I tell myself I don't have to make bad consequences for myself. For instance, I used to *know* that if I had a terrific day, I'd pay for it at night with a terrible anxiety attack. Well, I had to learn that I was setting my mind for it—all by myself. I didn't have to program myself to punish myself for having a good day.

"Finally, I learned to slow down and to get enjoyment from a nice, calm, small thing. Now, after a terrific thing happens, I deliberately get involved in a *small* nice happening, in order to slow me down. This way, I ease out of my intense feelings—and I don't wind up in a state of anxiety."

34

This Too Will Pass

Forty-nine-year-old Roxanne was a tall, thin, composed brunette. She looked self-assured, but her words revealed otherwise.

"I *always* let other people get to me," she moaned. "Last night, my boyfriend and I went over to my best girlfriend's house, where she lives with her boyfriend. I'm supposed to start work on a doctoral program in the spring. I'm also trying to get free-lance work while I'm going to school.

"The doctoral program is partly exciting, and partly boring. I already know and anticipate that. But I told Irene about my plans—she's going for another masters degree instead of going on for a doctorate—and she tore me apart.

"She told me I might find the doctoral program too boring, and that the free-lance work was too much for me. She also said I should just go out and get a job. She told me I should learn to structure my life better, and that, if I couldn't handle a structured job, what was I doing getting ready to go for a doctorate?

"But the worst thing of all was: She said all this in a very angry tone of voice and, also, there was a grain of truth in it—enough so that I got scared.

"I told my boyfriend about it on the way home, and he had some very sound suggestions. He said I ought to see from her behavior that it's more like Irene is talking about herself. Irene is probably angry with herself. She's jealous that I've got enough courage to go on for a doctorate while she's working on another masters.

"He also told me the fable about the ant and the grasshopper. The grasshopper hopped all summer while the ant worked for a goal—to store up food for the winter. The ant told the grasshopper he should get busy and plan ahead, but the grasshopper thought it was more important to have fun. Well, come winter, the grasshopper perished.

"My friend, Irene, is working on a rather useless masters—in a field where there are no jobs. And I'm going to work on a doctorate in a field where no one is unemployed. Sure, my program will be somewhat tedious at times. But all doctorates are, and I expect it, and I'm willing to deal with it.

"That's not all the bad part, though. After I got home, I got into an anxiety attack about all this. Irene was, after all, a good friend, and it upset me that there was so much animosity on her part without my having done anything to deserve it. I should have just dropped it, but I didn't.

"I did sort out the truth—*that* I will give myself credit for! The truth is that I *can* do doctoral work in addition to free-lance work. I can adjust my free-lance work to my studying. I can take as little or as much as I want.

"After next September, I'll be in such good financial shape, anyway, that I won't need to worry whether I get free-lance work or not. And that's when I do my best work, anyway—when I know I don't *have* to do it, but I just *want* to."

Roxanne took a deep breath, then continued. "How did I get rid of that anxiety attack? I told myself that all this will pass—that in a few months, I wouldn't be worrying about what Irene said. In fact, I wouldn't be worrying about it the next *day!*

"I told myself, 'This incident will pass.' It *is* an incident, not a crisis. This anxiety attack will pass, too—all of them have.

"What I didn't tell you was that earlier in the evening I had eaten one-fourth of a custard pie that we bought in the grocery store. It was in its box, not sold in the refrigerator section. After I ate it, I got nervous because it was made of eggs and was not refrigerated when I bought it. Several people reassured me that the preservatives in it make it all right. 'Just refrigerate any leftovers after you begin eating it,' they said.

"Well, I got kind of anxious about that. And I realized I often get anxious from this kind of thing. But, instead of getting into a full-blown anxiety attack over Irene and her petty opinions and jealousies—and over the pie—I decided the worst that could happen would be this: I would throw up or have diarrhea. Irene could be right in some aspects, and I may have to back off and take on less free-lance work—or drop it altogether—while going for my doctorate.

"Either way, I figured this would all pass. Probably, nothing *dreadful* was going to happen—either as a result of the pie or as a result of Irene's dire bodings.

"Practically nothing is that important; most things just pass uneventfully.

"When I told myself that, everything did just pass. And the anxiety attack just withered away.

"I learned something from that: I can *choose* my attitude; I can *decide* not to pay much attention to anxiety attacks or to other people. A lot of things that happen or that people say will just pass away if I let them."

35

Building Up to an Anxiety Attack

"Do you get any clues which indicate beforehand when an anxiety attack is coming on?" I asked Mindy.

"I do!" interjected Sarah. "I've been noticing it lately. Last week, it happened for the first time. I woke up in the morning, feeling out of sorts. I had a coffee with sugar and cream, and it made me extremely nervous.

"I got into an argument with my ten-year-old daughter which got me too mad, and this left a residual of anxiety. I guess I felt guilt for getting into such a heated argument over her leaving her stuff laying around.

"Then, I didn't do anything to calm down. Instead, I got into my artwork, which is exciting, and I built up more adrenaline. I never gave my system a chance to get into slow speed.

"By the time evening came on, I had a full-blown anxiety attack. I really paid for that day.

"But, the next day, I noticed that if I made my thoughts and my actions center around calm things, I would calm down quicker after I got excited or angry. I kept doing that throughout my day, and that evening went fairly well.

"Then, the day after that, I forgot about my resolution and let my emotions go crazy. By the time evening came, I had already had a small anxiety attack and was preparing for a bigger one.

"But a thought came to me: Why should I *have* to 'pay' for my feelings? If I *decided* to be calm, maybe I could *become* calm. So I tried it. I decided that the evening was the beginning of my day, and that it would be good in spite of the mess I made of the daytime. And it was!"

"I know when they're coming on too, sometimes," said Sue. "When I have a resentment I can't get rid of, I can't seem to get calm. I stay shaken all day, and the night, then, is totally destroyed.

"But I've learned to get rid of small attacks, anyway. I say to myself, 'how important is it?' And, if it's a relatively little attack, I make a decision to drop it. Nothing is worth losing my peace of mind over. Oh, to be free of anxiety attacks! It took me a long time to feel this way but the pain was finally too much for me.

"I just ask myself if this particular situation will be important six months from now. If it probably won't, I totally drop it."

More people joined in the discussion. What *are* the things that build up to an anxiety attack?

1. Resentment seemed to be the number-one offender. This included resentment over not getting something which was rightly due, resentment about something someone else said which concerns you, and resentment for having to do something that you didn't want to do and don't think you should have to do.

2. Dwelling obsessively on unpleasant thoughts. (Most of the people in the group said that when thoughts became truly obsessive, when there was no

getting rid of them no matter how hard one tried, they could *feel* the anxiety starting to build up. But when they learned to let go and accept the thoughts, let them just wash right on over them, then they went away.

3. Getting too hungry, angry, lonely, or tired (this forms the acronym HALT). The people in group said that when they got too much from one of these categories, they became vulnerable to an anxiety attack.

4. Not being good to themselves. When more than four or five days went by without doing something wonderful for themselves, the tendency was to become a little depressed and have a concomitant anxiety attack. The "cure," though, was simple: go out and enjoy yourself—*regularly!*

Other positive ways of successfully dealing with stress and anxiety include:

1. Staying grateful. That seemed to help a lot of people when everything else failed. Helping those less fortunate seemed to keep them in the frame of mind which says, "What I've got (just a nervous condition) isn't so terrible, after all."

2. Letting go of old ideas. Being open-minded enough to truly listen to ideas which go against the grain of one's old, entrenched philosophical systems. If the pain is great enough, most people said, they'd listen to anything!

3. Saying the serenity prayer and really thinking about its meaning: "God, grant me the serenity to accept [the reality of] the things I cannot change; the courage to change the things I can [myself]; and the wisdom [the honesty] to know the difference."

36

Do You Think You're Different?

I have had many clients who, when they began therapy, doubted that anyone could help them. The one thing they had in common was the notion that they were "different,"—they were too sick, they were the worst case that anyone had ever seen. They thought the principles I told them about (principles embodied in this book) were too simple for them, for they were complicated people. I told each and every one of them that this is a simple program for complicated people.

Let me tell you about some of these "different" cases and how they were helped:

1. Katie was seventy-five years old. She was referred to me when she found she couldn't function well living alone, and had to start living with her grown children. She would live with one daughter in Ohio for a while, then reside with one in Baltimore. Everything went well with the daughter in Ohio. But that would only last for six months, because the family made a pact to divide their time. Katie then had to move to the daughter's house in Baltimore.

Here, she had to put up with things which annoyed her. There were two teen-aged boys in the house who were into drugs; the mother—Katie's daughter—was depressed most of the time herself; her son-in-law was angry much of the time; and even the cat seemed hostile.

Katie became the scapegoat. "Everything went wrong when you came!" her daughter would scream at her.

No one wanted to take the blame for the disintegrating family relationships. The daughter and her husband decided that Katie had to go into therapy. Katie wound up in my office.

"Frankly, I don't know why I'm here," she said. "I'm very unhappy but I don't have a choice where to live. It's either in their house or in a nursing home. And since my anxiety attacks are a direct result of living with them, I don't see how you can help me. Besides, I'm too old to change."

"Look, Katie, I have a hunch that you think there's got to be 'something wrong' with you in order to see a therapist."

She agreed.

"Well, that's a misconception," I said. "A popular one, but wrong. All it means is that you admit you've got a problem that's getting in your way, and you'd like some help with it because doing it yourself doesn't seem to be working. Okay?"

"That sounds better than saying I've got to be crazy in order to be here," laughed Katie.

"Well, people used to think like that, back in the 'Dark Ages.' But in the last twenty years, it's become much more fashionable to have your own therapist— almost as popular as having your own orthodontist!" I told her. Then I went on. "Let me ask you, Katie. Just for today, do you want to stay at your daughter's?"

"Of course. If I can work out something we can all agree to, fine."

"Well, you don't have to work something out that you can all agree to. What you *can* do is change *your* behavior. That way, the people around you will all change. The dynamics of the family work that way: one person just changes; he doesn't speak to anyone about changing, he just does it. Others start to notice it, and comment on it. They don't realize it, but they change accordingly. Old 'games' stop because one person isn't playing any more. Get it?"

"It sounds exciting," Katie said. "I'm anxious to get started."

Katie did get started. She learned not to react when the teen-agers told their tales of woe. She learned to remove herself from the room when the tension was unbearable, and get into reading or watching television or doing something enjoyable while in her *own* room. She learned not to feel resentment when she had to retire to her room, that it was *her choice*—she could choose to stay in a tension-filled atmosphere or go to where there was peace. In a word, she learned how to *detach*, lovingly, from a problem-filled family, and how to enjoy the good that was in each of them, individually. She found out that the key was to enjoy being with them when they were alone. When it was a group, a family, it was best being out of their way.

"I guess old dogs *can* learn new tricks!" beamed Katie.

"Older people can learn to change if they're uncomfortable," I agreed. "You might have twenty or thirty more years in which to live. Why not make them enjoyable?"

2. Sally Ann was a black woman who came to see me as a client, but was also reluctant. She was divorced, had a six-year-old boy who tyrannized the household, and had a job she hated. She wanted to be a model. She

159

had been in a two-year depression, worrying about money and feeling trapped.

First, I reassured Sally Ann that her problems were universal to women. I understand that they were exacerbated because she was black, but they were certainly not insurmountable. It was simply a matter of differentiating between the problems—identifying them, deciding what course of action to take for each of them, and making a hierarchy of behaviors to deal with them all. And then doing it.

Sally Ann learned to insist that her child obey her; she became consistent in her discipline. It took only three weeks to straighten out *that* headache. (She did have quite severe headaches about child-rearing, but her migraines and anxiety ceased.)

She enrolled in a modeling course, got a few extra jobs modeling at department store shows, and therefore got some extra money. She found out that what she really wanted to do for a living was to work as a "buyer," so she enrolled in a night course in merchandising and is now working as a buyer in a downtown store. She is making more money than before and is much happier. She's even got a boyfriend who loves to go to New York for weekends—she goes too, and shops and shops! (And her son stays home, happily and peacefully, with a babysitter!)

If you think you've got the biggest, worst problem on earth, with anxiety and exacerbating problems, see if following the principles and exercises outlined in this book won't help you learn how to get on the right track in solving your problems. It can point you toward solutions that *lead to serenity*—whether this entails seeing a therapist for a short while, talking to your local clergy, or using the tools in this book so that your anxiety attacks and worry about problems can be overcome.

37

Beyond Survival

Life is, and should be, much more than just coping. You can be as happy, every day, as you make up your mind to be.

So, you've got anxiety attacks? They last about two hours of your day? You're awake sixteen hours—how do you feel during the rest of the fourteen hours? Anxious about the anxiety attack coming on? Waiting for the other shoe to drop?

This is where acceptance comes in. If you can learn to say to yourself, "When and if an anxiety attack comes, I'll accept it. But for right now I'm going to enjoy myself," then there's a good chance that anxiety attack won't even come!

There are a few ways to learn to make your life pleasant—instead of simply coping.

Just for today:

1. Live through this day only. Do not tackle all of life's problems at once.

2. *Decide* to be happy, no matter what happens. If you reflect on this regularly throughout your day, you'll get used to this attitude! Particularly if you're sick and tired of being sick and tired of anxiety!

3. Try to adjust yourself to what is; stop trying to adjust everything to your own desires. Decide to take things as they are and adjust *to them*.

4. Exercise your body: Eat right; work on one healthy thing, physically—just for today.

5. Study something that will require mental exertion—something that will enrich your life.

6. Do something for someone and don't get found out; it'll make you feel wonderful, inside.

7. Decide to be agreeable. Be liberal with praise. Decide to be an asset to this earth, and to other people, just for today.

8. Make a list of all the things you have to do today, and cross them off one-by-one as you finish them.

9. Relax and meditate for one-half hour.

10. Try to be unafraid, just for today. If you can't do this for a whole day, then try it for five minutes. Or, if necessary, take one minute at a time.

Try doing one of the above ten suggestions at a time for each of ten days. Add to the list as you find you are able to do so. The more of them you can do, the better you'll feel.

Appendices

Appendix A

Getting Help

If you are looking for a counselor, you may call the author of this book, Toby Rice Drews, for counseling. Her phone number is (301) 243-8526 in Baltimore.

If you would like to join Alcoholics Anonymous, Pills Anonymous, Narcotics Anonymous, Valium Anonymous, Overeaters Anonymous, Al-Anon, Al-Ateen, Neurotics Anonymous, or any other self-help group, call the telephone operator in your area for the number. These groups will give you meeting schedules and free literature.

If you cannot find the number for any of the above, consult a local chapter of Alcoholics Anonymous. They may be able to help you contact someone who may know of the organization you are looking for.

For further information, a free catalog of educational aids, or for personal counseling, write to:

Narcotics Education, Incorporated
6830 Laurel Street, N.W.
Washington, DC 20012, USA
(202) 723-4774

Appendix B

Suggested Readings

Drews, Toby Rice. *Getting Them Sober*. South Plainfield, New Jersey: Bridge Publishing, Inc., 1980.

Nudel, Adele. *For the Woman over Fifty*. New York: Avon Books, 1979.

Weekes, Claire. *Hope and Help for Your Nerves*. New York: Hawthorn Books, Inc., 1968.

Walker, Lenore. *The Battered Woman*. New York: Harper & Row, Publishers, Inc., 1979.

Dyer, Dr. Wayne. *Pulling Your Own Strings*. New York: Avon Books, 1978.

GETTING THEM SOBER

BY TOBY RICE DREWS

"... this book should be read by everyone ..."

—Abigail Van Buren (Dear Abby)

This is a totally new approach to problems surrounding alcoholism. There is no other book that offers such practical insights. It helps the alcoholic to have an 80 percent better chance to get sober and stay sober!

"This is an important book that will benefit large numbers of alcoholics. Its positive message so effectively presented will fill a great need."

—*Norman Vincent Peale*

"I will keep copies. . .next to the bench to give to families in crises. I recommend that other judges do the same for prevention and treatment of this horrible disease called alcoholism."

—*The Honorable Robert B. Watts*
Supreme Bench Judge, Baltimore, MD

Toby Rice Drews, M.L.A., The Johns Hopkins University, is a licensed social worker/counselor for the families of alcoholics. She is a professor of counseling and a free-lance writer and editor in New York City and Baltimore. She has written numerous articles, particularly on alcoholism and the family.

P460-6 Pocketsize
ISBN 0-88270-460-5
Topic: Families/Counseling
U.S. Price $2.95

A guide for those who live with an alcoholic.